CLAIR BAISLY

Cape Cod Architecture

Featuring the author's illustrated

index of architectural terms

PARNASSUS IMPRINTS, INC.

Orleans, Massachusetts

For Charlotte
and Shirley

Contents

Illustrations

Introduction

The house that you live in is a story book, of history and romance, of events and of people. To open this book to you and to make these tales come alive, to enable you to see through the walls, the windows and the doors into the colorful pageantry of the past, is the purpose of this book.

Your house, on Cape Cod or wherever it is, has an immediate past. This involves the who, how, when, where and why of its construction. For each house this is unique, a story to be researched and savored on an individual basis.

Your house also has a distant past, one that concerns its type and style. This is the story of the appearance, the floor plan, the facade and the detail. This tells us how the house's individuality developed and about the wonderful events that framed these happenings. The stories are shared by many houses and mirror the history of the times and the people.

And, finally, your house has an ancient past. This is the story of the components of the structure and how they originated with man's struggle to shield himself and his loved ones from the dangers around them. This relates to all houses.

Architecture is the great and honest recorder of human history. Our built environment is the direct and tangible expression of our needs, our interests, and our social, financial and religious patterns. It holds up our viewpoint as individuals and as a nation to scrutiny, to analysis and to comprehension. This is particularly clear to those who observe or live on Cape Cod today.

We read the present from our structures and we can also read the past. Without architectural remnants of bygone civilizations we would know relatively little about them.

The hot but patient passion of Egypt is most clearly told us through the tombs and pyramids and their contents.

We learn of Egyptian values — for example, that life was cheap but art was prized — and of their geology — wood and metal were scarce but building stone was available and it was moved by the labor of highly disposable slaves.

The political psychology and social philosophy of tyranny and terror, of fear and acceptance, are demonstrated in line, pattern, color and detail. We learn, too, from the wall decorations, of hunting and fishing techniques, of family relationships, of agricultural methods and, indeed, almost all that we know of these dramatic folk and their time.

The Greeks, whose civilization crested somewhat later, were far more democratic and their energies went into building towns for living people rather than a grave for a dead king. Here we see the basic philosophic difference between the two religions. The Egyptians put all their effort into the glorification and worship of one infallible ruler; the Greeks said their prayers to a large number of deities whose powers were tempered by human frailties.

Greek towns lay on sloping hillsides and were part of an undulating terrain, taking contour, view and defensibility into consideration. Public buildings, temples, theatres and markets were scattered across the landscape like the notes of a shepherd's pipe playing a gentle cadence.

The jagged outlines of the Egyptian pyramid defied nature, but the placid beauty of the Greek temple identified with it. What the Egyptians and the Greeks constructed proclaimed their viewpoint more clearly than any writing did.

The strong-minded and practical Romans left us voluminous writings about their civilization. Their architecture also gives us a straightforward synopsis of their thinking, needs and interests. The Romans built cities where they wanted them. The ground had to give way, water was made to cooperate, and the whole was laid upon a grid of common sense, with the buildings clustered for convenience and oriented to impress.

Even the canniest of the Romans had few secrets from the archaeologist who studies their constructions. Roman baths had richly mosaicked floors, with massively ceilinged rooms for hot, tepid and cold bathing. Bodily comfort was important to the citizens of Rome. Their baths, which included libraries and art galleries for relaxation, tell us of their sociability and taste.

The Romans were gregarious and urbane, with a class admiring wealth and power as the Greeks had not. The highly convivial Roman toilets, in the full out of doors, with zero privacy but plenty of landscaping, statuary and opportunity for conversation while seated, are history pages that are hardly otherwise available.

The wooden structures that now grace Cape Cod back yards as tool sheds were once two-, three- or even six-seaters, reminding us that privacy is a recent privilege. That these conveniences have walls demonstrates the necessity imposed by a climate more rugged than that of Rome and also an increasing sense of modesty.

While the view from the door may have influenced the placement of this little building, with vistas of water or sand dunes to be enjoyed, the art work is more pedestrian. There is no space here for statuary, but at least a girlie calendar or a color shot of a sports figure — for, after all, time, women and sports are important to Americans. Perhaps there is a copy of James Whitcomb Riley's poem "Hold Everything" to give us a view of the people and their era.

The resplendent cavalcade of man's architectural expression winds before us. The far end of it reaches back into the soft grays and browns of time that is older than man's memory of man's memory, with the colors and sounds and movement increasing as the procession nears.

There, stepping out with confidence, a little distance from the bulk of the parade, we see a Saxon dressed in skins with a pit saw over his shoulder. A few steps closer is a proud young man who must be a king. He holds with his left hand the hand of his yellow-haired queen, and in his right hand there is a precious bit of glass for her chamber window, a joy-present at the birth of their first son.

Still closer, coming into full light and color, is one of our own Pilgrims. Over his shoulder is a froe to make clapboards for his first serious Cape Cod home.

On the march is this vivid and exciting pageant of mankind, recording for us how our progenitors worshiped, how they sheltered their families, speaking to us of the geography and geology of their area, of their social and financial conditions, ever since man first domiciled himself with boughs torn from a lightning-splintered tree.

Your Cape Cod house is part of this picture. The progression of its structure and the component parts move along with our procession. The framing evolved during a thousand-year struggle to erect walls that would not be crushed by the roof. The picture window that brings such pleasure into your home was, in embryo, a wad of grass stuffed into a jagged hole in the side of the house.

The vast sweep of the psychology of architecture is a most revealing part of the story. Before us, too, is the simple tale of how it all happened in daily life — the slow, patient learning of how to cope with the environment, to deal with intractable materials and the needs of survival and, in time, to achieve a bit of comfort.

Architecture is not a frivolity like Baked Alaska, nor is it a personally expressive thing like fine art. Architecture is the practical manifestation of the immediate needs of a people for shelter, relaxation, worship and trade.

An artist, driven by a vision that he must make tangible, may, with a loaf of bread under his arm and his brushes in his hand, climb into an attic and pull the trap door shut behind him and there express his calenture. Years later a curious person might push open the trap door against the protest of its rusted hinges. The thread-covered bones in the corner are worth a momentary glance, but behold! — creations glow beneath the cobwebs and dust particles that have settled in the long-unbreathed air. Here is art, hallowed by the death of the author, to be publicized by the story of his demise, and shiny with the knowledge that the product is finite.

The viewpoint of the builder is otherwise. His eyes have a shorter range than our fanatical artist. The builder — or contractor or architect — needs a new truck. His kids want ski equipment and his wife wants to take a cruise. With him, of course. This mandates work that brings rewards within contractual scope. So he finds a buyer.

The builder and the buyer work toward a meeting of minds. To this meeting the buyer brings his needs and interests, and he offers, in return, money for their adequate fulfillment.

"Two bedrooms — one for me, one for my wife; give her the larger one. No guest rooms. We don't want relatives camping on us. The wife likes cocktail parties, so a big living room. No dining room; we eat at the TV with trays. And a nice TV room; I do enjoy the ball games. No upstairs. We are getting older. There is still one teenage son at home, and I can't *stand* that music, so fix a nice place over the garage for him. The outside — well, what do you suggest?"

The builder supplies his knowledge of costs, materials, and codes. Since the buyer does not have a clear idea of what the outside of his prospective house should look like, a skin of clapboards or shingles is wrapped around it and now it is called "Home."

Given the chance to study one such structure, the owner's instructions to the builder can be deduced by you, playing detective, and a social statement can be made about the owner and his family. A bit more looking will tell you something about the builder and his honesty, and also much about local building codes. The deeper you look the more you will learn; given a thousand such structures a good generalization can be made about life in the area.

Sometime when you are off Cape, go for a walk down a street in an area that is new to you. By using what you already know, you will be able to make some good assumptions about the history of the area and its residents, and have some fun at the same time.

For example, the church you see on the corner is immaculately kept; a wooden cartouche over the door gives a date of 1880. Since the building is painted two soft shades of gray, you might deduce that someone with a knowledge of architectural history is on the Board of Trustees (more about that later).

The church is on a generous lot, partly because land prices were low when it was built, but also because religion was important in family life then. There are community gardens at the back, bicycles cluster around a side door, and you decide it is a traditional church, active in the community, drawing from a stable neighborhood—a typical family church.

So down the street you go, noting the style, trim, quality of upkeep and landscaping of the large, roomy houses that were designed in the modes that are often lumped together under the misnomer of "Victorian."

In the next back yard you see an old privy, now converted to a tool shed. This was once a rural area and the present owners are more practical than self-conscious. There is an old garage, too small for a modern car but the owner, years ago, must have had a flivver.

Even the window shades are tattletales. This house has cream-colored shades with scalloped and fringed edges, and all over the house they are pulled to an exact horizon. At the next house we find shades at random levels. Most are green, one is white, and in an upstairs room—probably the kids' room—one is badly torn.

As you progress down the street you find the maintenance less careful. Yards are smaller and more tattered, and bird baths and yews give place to tricycles and rusty toys. One house has uncut grass, peeling shutters and in one corner of a window is a card: Room to Rent. Old age or illness may have wrought hardship here.

At the far corner is a grubby shop that sells newspapers and candy. Dead flies besprinkle the window displays and shreds of awnings flutter. But the door frame is elaborately carved and over it is a rich and colorful fanlight. The size and quality of plate glass say that for a previous generation this was an elegant and fashionable emporium. And then down the next street you glimpse a long-closed factory.

The people who have lived and loved and cried and died on this street do not know how plainly they wear their histories on their facades. We only invade their privacy with our minds, and then we go home and look at our own house with increased understanding.

There are few places that you will go where the works of man are not evident, and as long as you see structures, so long do you have food for thought and conversational dessert. When later we talk about the Cape Cod styles, our tapestry will be enriched and encrusted with inspiration and colorful with human drama, and it will express how clearly the past is part of the present.

Your Cape Cod house is a record of Cape Cod history, a story that begins in ancient times and brings the house-peeper into contact with the background, the growth, the people and the changing pattern of this our own Cape Cod land.

PART ONE

The house that you live in

CHAPTER ONE

Structural beginnings

And now, how did our Cape Cod architecture develop and grow? Its magical fascination unfolded from an embryo as awkward and primeval as the chrysalis of a butterfly. The idea of our cozy cottage first saw the light in England. It stowed away on board the *Mayflower* in the hearts of those homesick Pilgrim optimists through the months of a gray, greasy Atlantic crossing. Although there was no plumbing but the old oaken bucket in the corner and they had no dry socks to change into, the *Mayflower* passengers clung to their faith on board that small but sturdy vessel.

The idea of a home, both philosophical and tangible, sustained these early settlers through the first killing winter. Cold, hungry, sick and fearful, their belief in a light at the end of the tunnel of misery gave to some the extra strength that was needed to survive.

Within a few years they began to build their dream houses, which did not differ in basics from yours and mine. Floor, walls, roof, window, door and heat source — these simple components,

At the foot of succeeding pages is a visual glossary of architectural terms. They are arranged alphabetically for quick and easy reference.

3

like the notes of a musical scale, can be assembled in innumerable ways, and the resulting songs are unequalled in making a joyful noise unto the heart.

Seventeen years after the arrival of the *Mayflower* at Plymouth, some Plymouth residents and other folk more recently arrived in the (now) Boston area, came to "sit down" on Cape Cod, which had been so named by Captain Gosnold in 1602.

These people did not come to Cape Cod with wagonloads of furniture and tools and the wherewithal to build comfy domiciles. They struggled here on foot, walking over terrain that was pierced with streams, lifting weary knees over fallen logs, dragging wet feet through sloughs, unhooking their clothes from aggravating brambles and needing to sleep several nights on the way.

Records are few and tell of big events rather than small incidents. These Cape Cod folk were too busy surviving to keep diaries, and there was no corner post box for letters home, but we know that their first shelters, "Bothys" as they called them, were as primitive as had been those of the early Plimotheans.

Both those who settled Plymouth and Cape Cod went through a progression of construction that resembled, except for the time involved, a sequence through which their ancestors had moved long before. Their ancestors had taken thousands of years to go from boughs laid against a sunny bank to the cozy English Cottage. The early settlers on this side of the Atlantic went through the same chain of attempts, types and struggles within a generation or so. The English at Jamestown left written records which tell us of their primitive housing and of holding Sunday services under

A   **Acanthus**   **Accordion lath**   **Adze**

a torn sail draped over branches.

All over the world, primitive building has taken a similar pattern. When man moved from natural forms such as caves and trees, his earliest attempts at construction took a tepee shape, which is, in essence, "all roof and no walls."

"That this should happen under my roof." "She was left without a roof over her head." These and other familiar expressions tell us that traditionally "roof" is symbol for "home." There is good reason for this. Long before walls were accomplished there was a roof and the roof *was* home. It touched the ground on all sides. In Africa, Australia, Ireland, and for the Eskimo, the Amerindian and the South Sea Islander, the conical building was the first serious structure. Thus the sometimes scorned A-frame is our most historic form, the Alpha of construction, and it continues throughout our architectural pageant into the present day.

A cave is wherever you are lucky enough to find it, but a constructed shelter can be wherever you put it. This idea became important to our prehistoric hunter and gatherer as he wanted larger scope for his operations. He may also have wanted to get

Ancones   **Anthemion**   **Apron**   A

his women away from the old men at the communal cave. He did what the earliest settlers in the New World did a few thousand years later—he laid those boughs against an earthy incline.

To the early Briton the boughy lodging was new and thus exciting, but not secure against the wet and the wind, and man's natural itch is in the direction of innovative improvement. So the ends of the boughs were pushed into the ground for stability, the tops bent over and fastened together and small, pliable sticks were woven into the uprights.

Our builder had now made something that was more or less freestanding, therefore compatible with a number of terrains and, if need be, moveable—and he was off. But by no means running.

At the bottom the boughs were secured by stones, and dirt was placed between the stones. This marked the beginning, please take note, of masonry foundations. This progression is not conjectural. People in the British Isles were living in such all-roof huts well after the advent of photography (as photographic records show), and some people continued to do so into the present century. Some Laplanders today live in sod and stick conical huts. Tradition, that security which arises from dealing in something familiar, is the help-mate of culture lag.

Such Bothys could be covered with any available fabric, such as skins, turfs cut from that sunny bank or bundles of reeds. Whatever the covering, it would be laid on shingle-fashion, the lowest course put on first, each succeeding layer a little higher up and so on to the summit of the building, thus to shed the liquid elements.

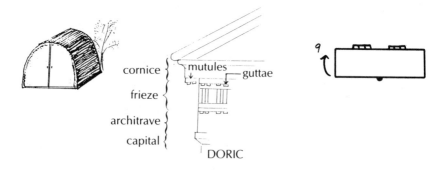

cornice
frieze
architrave
capital
mutules
guttae
DORIC

A   **Arched roof**   **Architrave**   **Awning window**

The turfs were placed grass side in, the better to hold the dirt, but with time grass would grow on the outside, too, along with weeds and cheery splashes of flowers.

This would bring the structure into close harmony with the landscape in texture, color and line. The family sheep or goats could wander up one side of the building and meander down the other, nibbling on the greenery.

Another way of foiling malicious weather was to weave small branches between the uprights and to cover the result with cob or daub, which is local mud mixed with animal hair and dung or dried grass. This is the famous wattle and daub of our early colonists, and of the rest of the world, and the ancestor of modern lath and plaster.

When gold was discovered in South Africa in 1886, and Johannesburg was invaded by fortune hunters, they found the miners living there in huts of wattle and daub, even as their progenitors had housed themselves a thousand years before. Good ideas have a way of sticking around.

When wattle and daub walls were further covered with turfs, the result was a snug, tight, easily warmed residence of considerable durability that could be built by the householder who had never taken "shop" in school. This type of dwelling sheltered Europeans for centuries and also helped the early New England settlers to survive the first rigorous winters. While such structures were strong enough for daily conditions, they might succumb to great storms, so a need for progress was indicated—but it was a long day and a stormy night in coming.

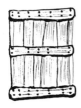

Barge board   **Bastion**   **Batten door**   B

If you wonder why old forms stayed around so long, consider this: for early building, and well into the Middle Ages, all but the very wealthy were their own housewrights. If you, right now, were homeless and cold and entirely dependent upon your own two hands and a few simple tools to provide for yourself and your family, what would you do to make a shelter? You would visit your neighbor, see how he had built, and do your best to copy. The result might be less than palatial, and speed, not innovation, would get priority.

Then of a fierce and starless night, with ropes of sleet lashing in mindless fury at nature and at man, your hapless family might be awakened by the top of the house landing upon their sleeping and upturned faces. The next day you would put it all together again, with the same resignation that we give today to pesticides in our food, drunken drivers on the road and rats in the sewer. There are always easy solutions, so we often don't take time for the hard ones.

Another challenge that the early householder took seriously was that of full head room. A man could not put up poles for his house any higher than he could reach unless he erected scaffolding, so there was full head room only at the center of the booth. Papa could stand — unless mama stood first. If she swung a baby rabbit by one skinny leg and asked papa if this was all the supper he could provide for a family of six, how much more effective was her scorn if he had to look up to where she stood taller than he.

And papa must have felt at a further disadvantage if, while hunkered over his rabbit bones, he looked up to see a growing

B   **Battered wall**   **Bay window**   **Belt course**

son tower above him as if to say, "You're getting weak, old man, and I don't like the way you boss me around." Whatever his motivation, man worked hard to add to the small amount of headroom in his all-roof hut.

Beyond doubt, mama made her contribution, too. We will not weasel around the use of the term "man." When he or she does his or her thing, we use the term "man" as a generic one, for reasons of simplicity and clarity, and it is here declared that the term includes both sexes and all age groups without reservation or discrimination.

Man tackled the height problem in several ways. For one solution he dug down inside the structure, leaving a wide rim of dirt that stabilized the house-poles and that could be used as a substitute for furniture (of which he had none anyway), for sitting, sleeping or eating.

Thus he achieved height in effect if not in fact. Many of our Cape Cod houses have dug-out cellars with dirt rims that are used as resting places for jelly jars, demi-johns of selected and delectable drinks and the baby's old play pen.

As another solution, man tried raising the structure on a knee wall of dirt and stones. Knee walls remain a common part of our Cape Cod houses today and are frequently used to define the low storage space under the eaves.

A third method was that of using curved branches, and this produced the most fascinating results of all, causing the eye-delighting camber of the old English cottage roof and of the New England bowed roof house, and giving birth in time to the modern

Bowed roof   **Brace**   **Bracket**   B

bowed roof replica.

A fellow who takes standard equipment and makes a radical departure, if that change is for the better, is considered a genius because his mind has leapt over several intervening steps. Perhaps the brilliant mind that achieved the next major improvement in the dwelling was a mother who had so many children that she didn't know what to do.

Whoever it was, praise to him or her. He took two sets of house-poles, put them several feet apart, laid a horizontal pole across the two sets of crotches and then covered the whole thing. Now everyone could stand, at least in a row.

Voilà, a bench mark in architectural progress, an inventive departure from the absolutely primitive tepee form that, whether in ice, wood, straw or mud has been built all over the world and is still being built.

Not as provocative as the wheel, nor as vital as the first seed dropped into well scratched soil, but nonetheless a Big Step. Now we have a ridge pole or ridge tree and we have gained another structural member of the house, one that is still with us, still part of our Cape Cod houses and part of most houses, for that matter.

In medieval times this ridge pole came to be called the "first" and it was considered the most supportive part of the house, holding up the rest of the frame. We who have come after Sir Isaac Newton take the falling of apples for granted, and we may have trouble understanding that people once believed that the top could support the bottom, but so they did believe.

Now around 50 B.C. those pragmatic Romans had overrun

B   **Broken pediment**   **Broken pediment**   **Bubble in roof**

Britain. Being practical people they consolidated their gains by careful planning. Wherever they conquered they opened up good lines of communication by means of fine roads. The roadbed was dug deeply, layered with large stones, then smaller stones, then fine gravel and all was topped off with good Roman brick. Time has destroyed most of these roads, but when they are found under the soil accumulation of centuries, they are remarkable for their workmanship.

The Romans did not build as elegantly in their colonies as they did at home, but in Britain they built pleasant villas with fine floors, good art work and, given the nature of the English climate, they probably installed central heat.

"Back home" they had central heat, seven-storey buildings, running water piped in, elevators, fire departments and other goodies such as sanitary flushing systems.

Around 450 A.D. the glue of the Roman Empire proved to have been spread too thinly. When the barbarians shook the Empire, it rattled and came unstuck. The Romans returned home and Britain was left to protect herself from the Jutes, Danes, Angles, Saxons and other invaders, who in time became assimilated — as the Romans had not — and who went on building with the same crude methods.

Sometimes we marvel at how slow people are to change and also at the vast discrepancies between the comforts of the rich and those of the poor. Wealthy people in Rome, fifteen hundred years ago, had luxuries that have not yet been achieved by all Americans. In England the monasteries — until Henry the Eighth

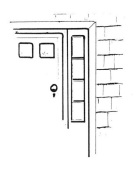

Bull's eyes   **Candle-snuffer roof**   **Cape Cod window**   C

dissolved them in the 1530s — had comforts that, while not equal to those of ancient Rome, did include sanitary flushing systems for wastes. And yet some Americans still use the old outhouse year-round.

The Romans did leave the pit saw behind and that was a great help in our progress. A pit saw was a long, two-handled affair that was used as follows: a log was laid across a pit and secured. One man stood in the pit, which should have been about seven feet deep. The other man stood on the ground and the two men pulled the saw back and forth between them along the length of the log. The fellow in the pit was soon up to his ankles and even higher in sawdust, and he was called the "under-dog."

The pit saw made it relatively easy to square a log by sawing off the round outer sides, so that when you built, your construction rested far more steadily on squared logs than it would have on round ones. So now we were blessed with the groundsill which still supports your house and mine.

The groundsill not only made for more stable construction but it raised the boards of the house off the ground, keeping them dry and thus longer lasting. Wood, standing vertically against the ground, will draw water up through the grain of the wood, a process devised by nature to draw water up into the growing tree. When this happens, rot sets in quickly. In ancient Crete, several thousands of years before Christ, this problem was noticed and the builders there set the supportive trees in doorways and court-yards upside down. This not only lessened water absorption but gave us the first ancestor of the Gothic arch.

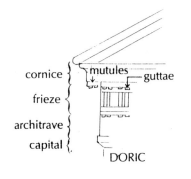

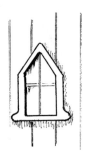

C   **Capital**   **Carpenter's Gothic window**   **Cartouche**

In early Britain the major supportive timbers of a house were often placed upon large flat stones. In early Plymouth and early Cape Cod building, vertical boarding caused the demise of many structures, for if the boards did not in themselves touch the ground, the seaweed placed around the building for insulation got wet and the snow unhelpfully rose high enough to add more damage.

Still another concept made its contribution to our British ancestors in their groping toward a stable home. This idea came with the Germanic invaders who built with five structural poles, one at each corner and one in the middle of the building. The center pole, which was the highest, was called the "king pole."

This center post was something of a navigational hazard, especially if you got up at night for reasons honorable or otherwise. Against its nuisance value had to be balanced the fact that it was the best thing yet devised to hold up the roof, something that folk really were anxious to get permanently off the ground.

This type of building had another plus, in that it could be extended with an additional king post and more side posts. Now tell me, please, where lie the bones of the genius who first stabilized the structure by laying a beam from the top of one side post to the top of the opposite side post, thus inventing the collar tie? No one asked him to speak at the British Housewrights' Convention in (perhaps) the year 640 A.D. or so. Nor was he knighted or even feted. But we use his remarkable invention every time that we build. The collar tie is basic to making anything stand upright and the concept will always be a universal necessity.

Groundsill, corner post, collar tie—all fastened together

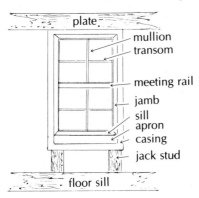

Casement window

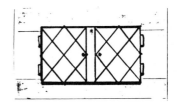

Casement window—glazed

C

with good oak pegs—and here we have the frame of our Cape Cod Cottage, our Cape Cod House and all the "Post and Beam" buildings that are having such a heyday now. These components were all achieved a thousand years ago, although Jack and Joan Poorfarmer continued to live in Bothys for centuries to come.

But that king post was still in the way, still tripping our feet when we hurried and cracking our skull at midnight. Then one day some anonymous hero, nursing the stubbed toes of the foot that had collided with the base of the king post, yelled in his native language—whatever it was and which we will at once translate for you—"Cut that fool thing off; we don't need it down here; let it rest on the collar tie. Oh dammy, I think my toe is broken."

So cut the fool thing off they did, and there it rests today, the dependable and highly supportive king post, a vital part of our home, and the father of all trussing systems, cathedral ceilings and basic roof structure.

The periods that we are discussing cannot be pinpointed on a time line. All aspects of human creation have some sort of a culture lag and few are more crazed with this problem than architectural history. Wherever people gather in numbers, where ideas and commerce move freely, there progress accelerates. In areas of less activity, there progress can mark time indefinitely.

And those who "have" in any area are in advance of those who have less, while "them as have nothin' " seem to stand still in all aspects of building and domestic comforts. So over all of our subject must be laid a three-dimensional grid of urban, suburban and rural, of wealthy, median and poor.

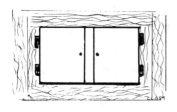

C   **Casement window–wood**   **Cat slide roof**   **Chicago window**

An example of culture lag is shown by referring to Alexander Graham Bell's most famous opus. My grandmother in New Jersey had a table telephone with a dial in 1930. Thirty years later on Cape Cod, I got my first dial phone, and in another twenty years my son in Nova Scotia went directly to dialing from the "Hello, Mabel, give me two rings on the line" hand-crank wall phone. And yet all during that time we were communicating.

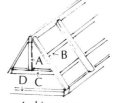

A. king post
B. purlin
C. collar tie
D. plate

Chimney pot   **Clerestory window**   **Collar tie**   C

CHAPTER TWO

Raising the roof for our Cape Cod Cottage in merrie England

R aising the roof often results in headaches; on the other side of the coin, not raising the roof probably resulted in even more headaches, so full head room continued to be a goal. The slight bow in the roof, which we mentioned before, did give a little extra head space, and it did not require straight members to build. It did create an arched effect and it was, indeed, handsome — with a gentle curve against the sky that has delighted the eye ever since.

Curved wood has had its appeal all through the years. Today a carpenter, after picking up a two-by-four and sighting along the edge, will discard it if it is bent or twisted. Modern quick-drying methods can distort lumber. But reaching back to the earliest wood construction in England and lasting through the 1700s in the Colonies and on Cape Cod, rafters, collar ties, wind braces and structural pieces were often curved, especially for those who could afford them.

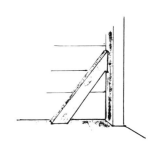

C   **Conical roof**   **Corbeling**   **Corner post**

Naturally bent wood is as strong as straight wood. Medieval man, quite innocent in the matter of physics, thought that curved wood presented both greater pull and greater thrust; after all, you remember, he thought that the "first" held up the house. The builder-architects of the great cathedrals may have had superior knowledge, but in those days communication wore lead boots.

Almost all wooded areas that we can find today have had some human interference in their growth pattern. Virgin forests hardly exist. Only there might we find a commercial quantity of naturally curved trees which result when mature trees propagate and the new generation, seeking the light and sun that they require, bend and twist in the hunger of their quest.

The profession of timber cruiser was an important one in the American colonies. His job was to take orders from clients who were going to build of wood, a vessel, bridge or house. The prospective builder would give the timber cruiser specifics as to the size and shape of bent wood that was needed for the bow of a vessel, the rafters of a house or the trussing of a bridge. Growing trees that fulfilled the requirements of curve and size would be located, and men would follow to fell the trees and deliver them to the builder.

Wood that is bent during natural growth will keep its curve throughout its lifetime. Wood that is bent by artificial means can return to its original shape by as much as fifteen per cent, and is therefore less desirable. As long as virgin forests remained, the timber cruiser performed his valuable function and supplied sturdy timbers for construction. When naturally bent wood was no longer

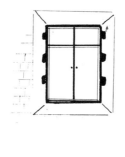

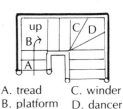

A. tread   C. winder
B. platform   D. dancer
A THREE-RUN STAIR CASE

Cornice   **Cruciform window**   **Dancers on stairs**   D available, other methods were used, as we shall see.

Cape Codders have always been strongly traditional people and they bowed the roofs of their houses almost without exception. The more substantial homes, especially on the Upper Cape, used rafters, collar ties and wind braces made from naturally bent trees. Many of these roofs are being destroyed because of a lack of understanding and insensitivity, but a few remain.

Most people, however, when building simple homes, cambered their roofs by an easy method, using an adze. An adze is a tool that was second only to the axe in the respect of the early settlers. Men boasted that they could even shave with their adze. This sounds like an awkward feat, to say the least, but their skill was of a high order and their pride was justified by their accomplishments. The blade of the adze is at a right angle to the handle, and the bevel is on the inside of the blade. The finest smoothing of wood was done with this facile tool.

The workman who wanted to bow the roof of his house would lay the rafter on the ground between his feet. Standing over it at midpoint, adze in hand, he moved backward, slicing off the wood until, arriving at the end of the rafter, it was thinner by one quarter of an inch for each foot of its length. He then walked forward, turned around and proceeded backwards, working from the middle toward the other end. A trained eye and hand could do this task at a rapid pace and, even after having measured hundreds of rafters all over the Cape, I am continually impressed by the precision these workmen achieved.

Today the modern builder, when constructing the modern

dentils

IONIC

D   **Dentils**   **Diapered shingles**   **Doghouse dormer**

bowed roof house, uses a skill saw to curve a shim which he places on top of a straight rafter, or he may use mechanically bent wood. In either case he bows his rafter enough to be clearly visible, which is about twice as much as our traditional Cape Codder did.

In ancient England the king's personal forests, carefully tended and preserved, had long been a source of good curved wood, and from here came the bows of important ships and the frames of significant buildings. A tree, split along its length by the pit saw, yielded a pair of matched rafters.

Sometimes the king, if he wished to signify his pleasure to someone who had done him a favor, would show his appreciation by sending the lucky fellow a tree or two from the royal forests. The recipient would then use these curved members to build or to add on to his Hall. Proud of the honor done him by his king, he might put the symbol of the pair of rafters on his coat of arms. To this day we use this mark, now turned upside down, as an emblem of rank — the chevron.

The etymology of architectural terms is fun to pursue. "Chevron" is the French word for "rafter," and *Webster's* defines it as "1. a beam or rafter; 2. a heraldic charge resembling the barge board of a gable; 3. a distinguishing mark of rank consisting of two bars meeting at the middle."

Other terms for the curved rafter were "couple," that is, a couple of members resulting from a single tree, and "cruck." Cruck is also used to designate the form of earlier raftering that sprang from the groundsill rather than from the plate.

During the early medieval years when the roof was, literally,

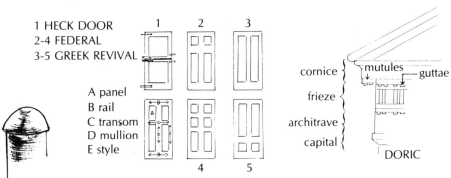

1 HECK DOOR
2-4 FEDERAL
3-5 GREEK REVIVAL

A panel
B rail
C transom
D mullion
E style

cornice { mutules — guttae
frieze {
architrave {
capital {
DORIC

Domed roof   **Door types**   **Doric capital**   D

getting off the ground and house framing began to include low, exterior walls, there were trees available that could provide, in a single piece, both the side post and the rafter. The side post was made with the trunk of the tree and the rafter by a strong, suitably curving branch that sprang from the main trunk. When such trees became scarce, the two parts — post and rafter, found separately — could be mortised together.

The chronology of these methods differed from place to place, but the concepts are universal, failing only where trees were not available. The knowledge is documented by old buildings that were torn down while the camera was around to record the anatomy.

On Cape Cod, where tradition and poverty were more determinative than the stylistic ambitions that resulted in so many changes off-Cape, hundreds of bowed roofs remain today. Most of these were built with the adzed rafter, a few with the naturally bent tree. Long after the curve contributed any possible help in adding head room, when houses were two or more storeys high and the rafters were concealed in the attic space, the process of bowing was maintained as an essential that added little work but much subtle beauty.

In a few instances the camber was readily noticeable, resulting in what is generally recognized as the bowed roof house, the curve being about one half inch per foot of rafter. In the far larger majority of cases the curve is one quarter inch per foot of rafter. These bowed roofs are unnoticed by most people but appreciated by observing house-peepers. They are a wonderful tribute to the manual dexterity, the cultural pride and the keen eye of the Cape

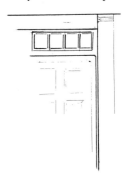

D   **Dutch gambrel roof**   **Eyebrow window**   **Fanlight**

Codder. Momentum and affection carried this lovely line over into the Greek Revival of the 1800s.

Examples can be found by standing at the corner of the building and sighting up at the raking cornice of the roof. A gentle rounding will be seen. Proof positive is achieved by going up into the attic and measuring the depth of the rafters from the eave to the apex of the roof.

If the depth of the rafter changes about one quarter of an inch for each foot of length — so that a rafter sixteen feet long and eight inches thick at the eave end, and ten inches thick at midpoint, is again eight inches thick at the apex — you have the genuine article in hand.

The roof is a vulnerable area, subject to fire, powder post beetles and rot from leaks. Roofs are often replaced without regard to the original camber, as photographs, drawings and verbal accounts attest. So while hundreds of the gently curved roofs remain, hundreds have been lost, but the conspicuous bow is still recognized and preserved.

The subtle bow had a revival on Cape Cod in the 1930s and 1940s, and many householders who built in those years point with pride to the barely discernible curve of their roof and boast that only they and their builder know about the camber.

Again in the 1970s the fashion took on new life and a larger geographic scope, with a number of building companies offering a bowed roof house. The amount of bow is generally around six- or seven-sixteenths of an inch and the arc is often achieved by bending a batten and drawing around it.

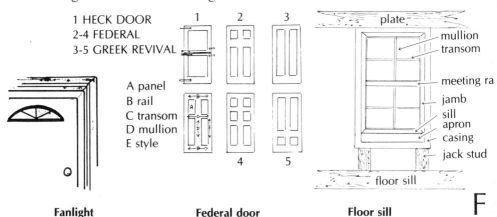

1 HECK DOOR
2-4 FEDERAL
3-5 GREEK REVIVAL

A panel
B rail
C transom
D mullion
E style

plate
mullion
transom
meeting ra
jamb
sill
apron
casing
jack stud
floor sill

Fanlight   **Federal door**   **Floor sill**   F

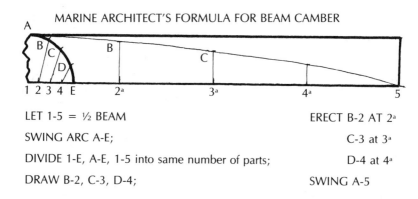

MARINE ARCHITECT'S FORMULA FOR BEAM CAMBER

LET 1-5 = ½ BEAM

SWING ARC A-E;

DIVIDE 1-E, A-E, 1-5 into same number of parts;

DRAW B-2, C-3, D-4;

ERECT B-2 AT 2^a

C-3 at 3^a

D-4 at 4^a

SWING A-5

Many people relate the bowed roof to the bottom of a ship, but this is not an accurate relationship. The main deck of a vessel may curve at a quarter inch per foot and that of a fishing boat or yacht may curve at a half inch per foot, but bottoms are different.

In order for a boat to move successfully through the water and to stay upright, every pair of its ribs has a different curving, narrow at the bow, swelling amidships and tapering off at the stern. Ships' ribs, moreover — for strength and in order to achieve the double curve that is required — are made of many small pieces of wood, bolted together in what is called double-sawn framing, and these could not be assembled into rafters. Deck beams — well, maybe.

The naval architect uses a formula for cambering deck beams, as shown in the illustration above. This formula can also be used for cambering a rafter if you don't want to do it by eye.

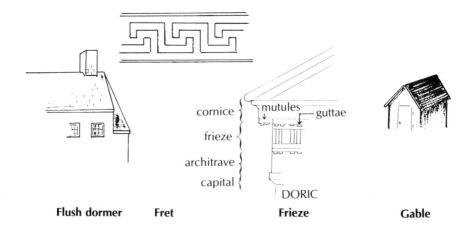

cornice

frieze

architrave

capital

mutules

guttae

DORIC

F   **Flush dormer**   **Fret**   **Frieze**   **Gable**

CHAPTER THREE

The fenestration of the Cape Cod Cottage and the Cape Cod House

The fenestration, that is, the placement of the doors and the windows of a house, is vital to the appearance. We look with warmth and affection at the Cape Cod Cottage or the Cape Cod House whose facade has the traditional pattern of doors and windows. When we see a house whose facade has been changed, it lacks something that we enjoy. Simplicity, regularity and proportion are invaluable ingredients.

The one opening in the earliest Bothys was the doorway. We use the word "door" today to include the opening, its closure and the door enframement too, but once there was the hole in the building and the door was there to close the hole.

Years and years ago the early door closers were made of a bunch of brush, or an animal hide or a stick-frame filled with wattle and daub. Still later there was a board, unhinged, and the door hole was uncovered by moving the door to one side. The door was then leaned against a stake that was placed nearby to receive it.

Gable on hip   **Gable on shed**   **Gable with shed**   **Gambrel**   G

Cape Cod doorways of the 1600s and the 1700s were often six feet high or less. People tended to be a little shorter than they are today, and those tall people who cracked their head on your lintel because they did not duck did not sue you but instead blamed themselves for forgetting to duck. In England, hundreds of years before, doorways were often four or five feet high, not because people then were that much shorter, but to conserve heat. For the same purpose, an Eskimo enters an igloo on his hands and knees, through a tunnel.

When houses began to be framed and the frame was strong enough to support the weight of a door and to withstand the stress of in-and-out traffic, the door was hung. Leather hinges were used early both in England and on the Cape. These were replaced by wooden hinges, which were an improvement because they were less apt to sag. Still later the village blacksmith, standing in the shade of a chestnut tree and flexing his muscles, while eyeing the girls who passed by to watch him flex his muscles, made metal hinges for doors, and they were often long strap hinges. Some of these can still be found in old Cape houses, relegated to the attic door, along with the hand made latches which on the downstairs doors have been replaced by those wonderful new knobs.

What an exciting day it was when all those old-fashioned handmade latches and hinges could be chucked into the back of the barn and doorknobs bought and fastened into place. Some folks filled up the holes left in the door by the removal of the latches and other folks just left the holes there. We see these apertures today and sigh and go out to the barn to scratch around

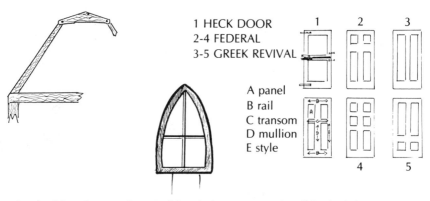

1 HECK DOOR
2-4 FEDERAL
3-5 GREEK REVIVAL

A panel
B rail
C transom
D mullion
E style

G   Gambrel framing—early   Gothic window   Greek Revival door hopefully. Oh, to find those wonderful handmade fasteners with their imperfections and irregularities! Fashion is a stern master.

When a board wide enough to cover the entire door opening was available it was used. When only smaller pieces were handy they were strapped together by pieces placed at right angles. The outside of the exterior doors would get the vertical boards in order to shed the rain better, with the horizontal pieces used on the inside. A thicker board would be used at each outer edge, one to hold the hinges and another to provide stability for a latch. We call these batten doors.

Latches, like every other part of our house, "developed" and the progression of old England was followed, in a shorter time frame, in New England. We can still find Cape Cod houses whose front door is barred by a long stick of wood that crosses the entire door and whose ends fit into slots in the door jambs. This seems to have been about the earliest fastening both here and in England.

As door frames became heavier and hinges became stronger, the bar was shortened and it went just from the door style at the opening into the nearer jamb. This short piece was easily mislaid, and what a nuisance that was when the man of the house wanted to go to bed and couldn't find it — "Where is the cussed thing? If that dog took it — " It soon came to be fastened to the door and it slipped down into a hook-shaped piece that was attached to the nearer jamb.

Some place along the line — authorities differ about when — a latch string was passed from the inside of the style through a hole in the door so that the latch could be opened from the

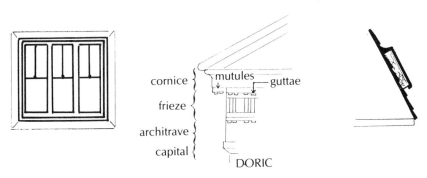

cornice } mutules
            guttae
frieze }

architrave }

capital {
        DORIC

Grouped window   **Guttae**   **Hatch in roof**   H

outside. When retracted, the latch string effectively closed the door against subsequent arrivals. "No, I won't leave the latch string out for you, my son. You knock when you get home."

Looking at the batten door suggests how door paneling developed. Paneling at first was simple, but with time it came to be stylized and style-related. The six-panel door is the one most frequently found on the Cape, especially for exterior doors. This type has two small panels at the top, two somewhat larger below, and two long panels at the bottom. This type is derived from Federal motifs.

The Greek Revival door shows either two panels running the entire length of the door or two almost as long as two shorter ones near the bottom. Doors with two equal square panels are found with any type of interior and remind us most clearly of the batten door.

The doorway has always been a true essential of a domicile, but no other aperture was considered necessary for a long time. But then someone made a small hole in the wattle or earth shelter. It was an insignificant hole, a few inches across, so that he — or she — could see what was happening outside. Was she coming yet? Was she talking to him in the yard? Over the years the derned thing grew, in spite of growls from folk with a draught across the back of the neck, in spite of verbal opposition, in spite of rain trickling in. That cussed hole, in time, became those great sliders that give you such a grand view of the garden and of the bird feeder.

The original hole — and we are speaking of a thousand years

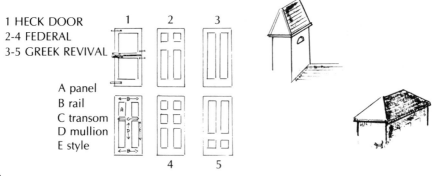

1 HECK DOOR
2-4 FEDERAL
3-5 GREEK REVIVAL

A panel
B rail
C transom
D mullion
E style

Heck door   Helm roof   Hip and ridge

H

ago — was plugged by a wad of grass and such primitive windows were still in use in rural areas of the British Isles in the early 1800s. Holes of varying heights followed, because curiosity is contagious, and if you can peek, why can't I? Detractors argued that the hole gave ideas to unwanted guests, for here the house was especially vulnerable. The term "housebreaker" is an old one and literal, too. An unfriendly person, wanting to get into a Bothy, just broke in the walls.

But good ideas will persevere, and curiosity triumphed over discomfort. The day arrived when the hole had enough prestige to be closed, not just by crumbly turf, but by a board. As did our door, the board soon acquired a fastening, and for the same reason that the door latch was attached — the board was so easily lost. Mama took it to chop up some chickens; the kids used it for defense in a snow ball fight; papa coming home late threw it on the fire. We are not being merely facetious. At the Battle of Hastings, in 1066, the beleaguered Saxons took down their windows and doors and used them as shields.

So the board was fixed at the side or at the top and later it was put on a track which allowed it to slide horizontally. This wooden closer with any of three types of fastening, top, side or sliding, can still be found on Cape Cod fishing camps, between kitchen and dining room on older houses (for handing dishes and food back and forth), on storage sheds and summer camps, and also on your local ice cream parlor. Translated into glass, such closers are found everywhere today, and are considered quite elegant as casement windows, transom windows and glass walls.

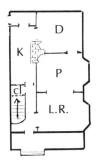

Hip and valley   **Hipped roof**   **House plan—side hall**   H

Good ideas won't quit.

The casement window in which first one and later two leaves open outward has had the longest run. It began a thousand years ago in wood. Changed to glass it graced our Cape Cod homes for the first hundred and fifty years. Recently it has been revived to give a spurious ancient air to modern homes and to quaint restaurants such as Ye Olde Colonial Fast Food Take Out Inne.

But before it was glazed, the casement had an alliance with some oiled fabric. "Bring paper and oil for your windows," our first settlers wrote home. This combination did not retain much heat, but it let in some light and the wooden board was added in bad weather.

Alas, the course of love is seldom smooth. Glass came along and the window hole fell madly in love with this shiny stuff and told the oiled paper to get lost, a better bed fellow had been found. The resulting happy association is still with us and has not yet been improved upon.

Glass is one of man's most astonishing and useful creations. Its advent caused the wooden shutter to be relegated to the outside of the house. In time the once-essential shutters became merely decorative and were adorned with cutouts of sailing ships, Scotty dogs and tulips. Today shutters are often plastic and fixed in place as part of the patterning of the facade.

But the shutter was also let inside again as the boxed interior shutter that added charm and privacy to homes in the Revolutionary era. Now they are back once more, not boxed into the window frame this time, but folding back neatly.

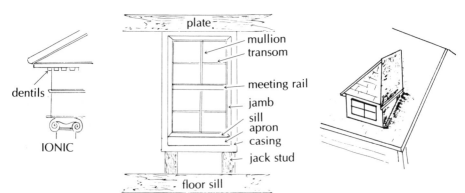

Ionic capital   **Jamb**   **Jerkin head roof**

The wedding between glass and the window hole was that of two late bloomers from opposite sides of the railroad track. The window was a lowly contrivance, regarded with suspicion and dislike. It brought in the poisonous outside air, it introduced spits of rain and sparkles of snow and it slipped a knife blade of cold down between hunched shoulders.

Precious glass, made with trouble in tiny amounts, had been prized as a jewel, desired by kings, and when it was fashioned, during the 1100s, into the awesome visual banquet that glorified Gothic cathedrals, it was escalated into worldwide acclaim and admiration.

Window hole and glass, how they sang in duet, how the two, hand in hand, revolutionized buildings, both within and without. A house on the outside ceased to be merely a lump of natural materials, indigenous in color and texture, with little to set it apart from its surroundings. Now a house glittered in spots, suggesting treasures of love and comfort within. When the sun was low it had splashes of gold to set it apart. The consciousness of these shining bits brought about the genesis of fenestration, the deliberate planning of the facade.

Light, brought within, lengthened the day and changed the interior into a place of relative cheer and spirit. Work could now be accomplished when the door was closed against the weather. The house became a home. Sunshine now pointed up unwholesome corners that the firelight had long overlooked and slowly the window inspired an interest in the interior appearance.

Early windows, when glazed, were fixed — that is, they did

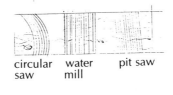

circular   water   pit saw
saw   mill

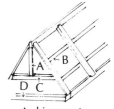

A. king post
B. purlin
C. collar tie
D. plate

Jetty   Kerf marks   King post   K

not open—and then they followed the development pattern of the parental shutters.

Glass came in small pieces and a number of pieces had to be fastened together to make a whole. And to fill a hole. The holding material into which the glass bits were fastened was first lead and later wood, and the pieces were diamond-shaped because sloping angles shed water more readily than horizontal ones.

Snow and rain did not lie long on the diagonals that held the glass in place. Gothic churches, with their emphasis on windows, had window hoods and labels further to shed moisture, and these remain hallmarks of the Gothic styles (as we shall see later), as do the weathering surfaces at the angles of walls. But we are not chronicling the stories of churches, palaces and mansions, those great stone explorers in enclosing space. This is the humbler tale of wooden construction, the architectural steerage, so to speak, that grew with time and the accumulation of knowledge to stand tall and beautiful in its own right.

A younger cousin of the so-popular casement was the cruciform window. In this type the window is divided in half vertically and about two thirds of the way up horizontally, the dividers forming a cross. Either the upper or the lower part opened and the other part was generally fixed.

The glazed bay window, which seldom opened, was long a fixture in the English nobleman's hall. During the 1400s, glass windows began to be a standard part of better homes, often in the form of an oriel, and by 1700 all but the poor accepted a window as a natural part of the house. (A bay window springs

Label   **M roof**   **Mansard roof**

from the ground; an oriel is cantilevered from the wall.)

A little after 1600 the sash window appeared in England and within a hundred years the American colonies had workmen who could cope with this new and more complex form. The universal acclaim accorded to the sash window coincided with the English Renaissance, whose architectural expression we call Georgian. Without the sash window, the Georgian style would have been far less effective because Georgian is an intellectual style whose facade is carefully planned and is based on a module of whole numbers. The sash window is easily made in the Georgian proportions of a window whose height is twice its width, and opening the sash window does not disturb the appearance of the facade.

The casement type is limited in size because, opening outward, it offers surface resistance to the wind. The sash window moves up and/or down and can be of any size for which glass is available.

The sash window slides vertically and sometimes opens its upper part and sometimes its lower part and sometimes both. The lower-opening type prevailed for homes, although to this day the upper-opening sort is used in schools and gymnasiums, operated by a janitor at the end of a long pole.

Sash weights, placed in the frame, were used in England after 1700 and came here within another hundred years. They made the window more stable when open.

When only the lower half opens, the window is known as the Guillotine window. This is either propped open with a stick or held open by means of a small catch at the side of the frame.

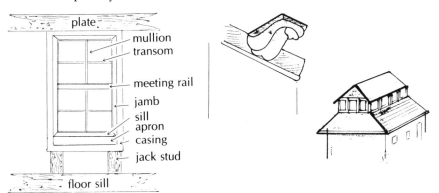

Meeting rail   **Modillion**   **Monitor roof**   M

These various fasteners are dependable when the weight of the window is pressing down on them, and they are released by a slight upward motion. So when you lean out of the window to tell the children to get the dickens out of the flower beds, a tiny push of your shoulder or head can get the back of your neck soundly whacked. WHAM. The Guillotine window, which has earned its name time and again, gleefully reaffirms its right to the title in hundreds of older homes that retain it, many of which are here on Cape Cod.

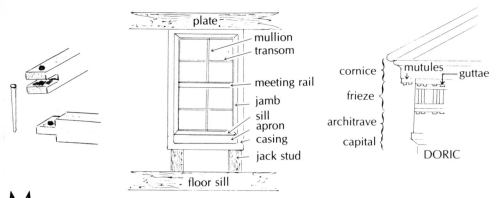

M   Mortise, tenon, and pin   Mullion   Mutule

CHAPTER FOUR

How our Cape Cod floor plan developed

T he development of floor plans is of value in helping us understand our Cape Cod Cottage and our Cape Cod House. If we go to England and visit a sprawling seventeen-room mansion, which is called The Hall, we may assume that hiding somewhere, possibly near the center of the building, is one room, very old, where long ago everyone slept and ate and which they called The Hall.

Similarly today when we see a Cape Cod Cottage or Cape Cod House, and near the door is a neat little plaque with a date that says 1735 or something like that, we assume there may be a room, a single room that was the original house. And guess what, the original owners called that room The Hall.

In England, five hundred to fifteen hundred years ago, The Hall was usually rectangular, with a dais at one end for the Man of Importance and his Lady. Here they celebrated their wedding night, slept, had children and died without ever realizing that they

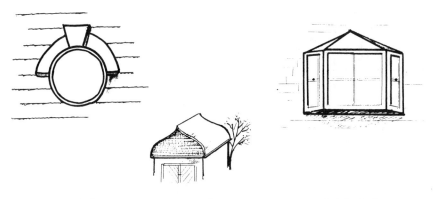

Occulis window   **Ogee roof**   **Oriel window**   O

had no privacy.

Down along the sides of The Hall the servants slept. Each had his own space, sometimes designated by a stone, and his own coat to wrap up in. Nothing else was his — or hers.

A low wall divided the human habitation from that of the animals, who also contributed warmth to the establishment. That they made other contributions was not of much moment. The animal noises could hardly compete with those of dog fights, children crying, the master and friends when drunk, and anything else that you can imagine when twenty or so people are living in one room.

Odors — ? Well, when no one in The Hall has bathed since he fell into the horse trough as a child, when — without benefit of a laundromat — clothing was used throughout a lifetime and then willed to the next generation, and when fresh air was considered dangerous and water even more so, who minds a few goats?

Focus is the Latin word for "hearth," and as a source of light and heat and cooking, the hearth has always been the focus of the home. The hearth fire in ancient times was simply made, much as you would make a beach fire today, with a low wall of soil around it. The hearth itself was the dirt of the floor, the location slightly off the center of the Hall and not near the side of the structure. The fire gave generously to all of its warmth, sparks and smoke.

The central hearth had its dangers; the dog might chase the cat too close, children could fall into it, loose clothing was vulnerable. The hearth acquired later a stone skirt, but what it needed most of all was a chimney.

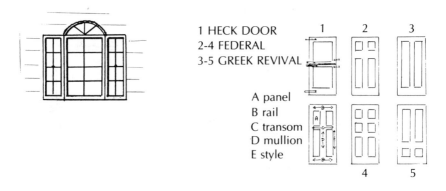

1 HECK DOOR
2-4 FEDERAL
3-5 GREEK REVIVAL

A panel
B rail
C transom
D mullion
E style

P   **Palladian window**   **Panel**

Stone castles had chimneys, but our concern is with the development of the simple cottage that is our architectural background. The owner-builder worked in weak, flammable stuffs and had no access to the methods and materials of the wealthy Earl on the hill. It may be hard for us to accept the poverty of pocket and mind of the English small landowner and the peasant who followed him in architectural progression, but it was then an unquestioned way of life.

Consider the smoke. If smoke makes you choke, think of living in a single room with an open, unflued fireplace. A hole in the roof could help, but it had to be set off center or the rain would put the fire out. And smoke is willful.

Generations of folk were born and died in houses that had no smoke outlet at all. "Black houses" they called them in Scotland and the thatch above was truly a mass of inky soot. The walls were pretty pitchy too. It is amazing to contemplate how long-suffering our ancestors were, how slow to change, how sturdy to survive. And if your ancestors were not English, they were subject to the same conditions in France, Scandinavia, and everywhere else, unless they lived where the door stood open all year round.

By the time our settlers had arrived at Plymouth, the English hearth had migrated to a corner of the Hall, against the flammable wall. That is one reason why so few houses remain to us today.

Used as a fuel, peat gives a low flame, but the temptation to use high-flaming wood in this chilly new England climate must have been great. All those trees were lying in the yard, the result of clearing the land, the house was flimsy — "Oh, I'll be careful, but

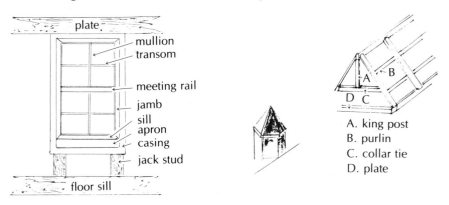

Plate   **Polygonal roof**   **Purlin**

P

EARLY SMOKE VENTING
1. The heck-door
2. An early louver, from the French word, "l'ouvert," an opening.
3. A Black-house

I am chilled through. And baby is sick. Just this one piece of wood, no more."

There was no fire engine when the thatch caught, no high school to go to for shelter, and soon nothing left but ashes.

We speak of English customs because there is a direct and obvious link between Cape Cod types and those of old England, but the patterns and progress are much the same the world over, with differences for climate and time.

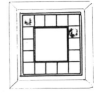

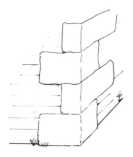

P

Pyramidal roof   **Queen Anne window**   **Quoin blocks**

Post and lintel construction is ubiquitous. The first single primitive room with later additions, the central hearth, the bowed roof—these are to be found in every culture at some point in the development.

The entrance door to our English Hall was at the end of the room at right angles to the dais. In time a screen was placed next to the door to lessen the impact of the wind on the fire when the door was opened. When the time came for the animals to be placed outside in their own structure, the part of the house that they had occupied became storage space, a pantry for dry goods and a buttery for wet ones. "Wet" included milk, cream, butter, cheese, beer, wine and similar things. Early Cape Cod merchants sold wet or dry goods, but the meaning changed until "dry goods" indicated clothing and fabrics, and wet as a term was dropped.

We will now add one room and then we will recognize clearly our dear friend, the Cape Cod Cottage. This addition was the Parler (sic). We spell it "Parlor" now, but we got the name from the French word meaning "to speak" and the room was created for just that, a quiet place to go and talk with family or guests, away from the hubbub of the Hall. Since this room was the perk of the householder, it opened off his dais and was the first suggestion of PRIVACY to add dignity to our picture.

This Parlor did not remain an extrusion on our early English home but became an integral part of the floor plan, and when walls between the two rooms were sturdy enough, they could share a chimney and hearths. With this added comfort the Parlor became as popular as the Hall.

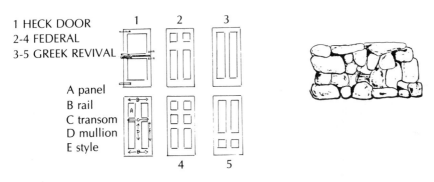

1 HECK DOOR
2-4 FEDERAL
3-5 GREEK REVIVAL

A panel
B rail
C transom
D mullion
E style

Rail   **Random rubble**   R

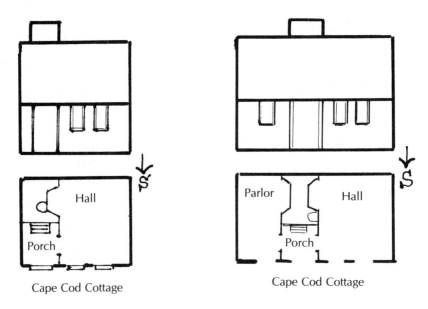

Cape Cod Cottage

Cape Cod Cottage

Under the effervescent conditions of the medieval home, life soon boiled over into every corner, and though further rooms were added, room use was undifferentiated. Cooking, sleeping and all domestic happenings took place in all rooms according to need and convenience. This freedom of use prevailed through much of the first two hundred years of American life until a home here was sufficiently commodious that the Parlor could be set aside for special occasions.

Those sturdy people who settled Cape Cod in the mid 1600s came with a carrot before their noses. First or second hand, they all knew about the farmhouse that had developed in the affluent

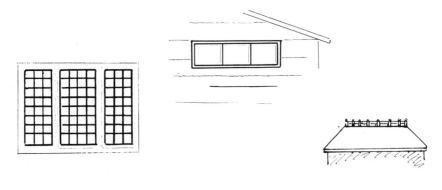

R   **Regency window**   **Ribbon window**   **Ridge comb**

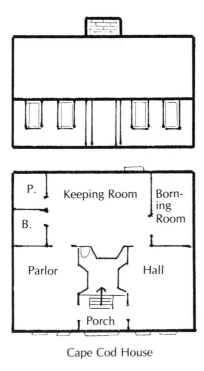

Cape Cod House

farming area of East Anglia from the components whose history we have been tracing in these pages.

Oh, what a carrot, cultivated by a hundred generations of home-hungry Britons, fertilized and watered by their tears, hopes and mistakes, this farmhouse had become, in the English 1500s, to be an object of veneration and desire. Now, on this side of the Atlantic, its idealization was about to blossom into something that we still cherish.

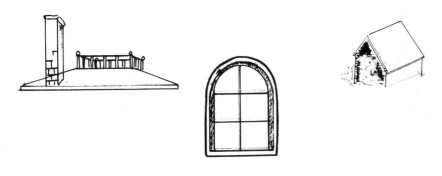

Roof comb   **Round-headed window**   **Saltbox roof**   S

Truly, the farmhouse then had no kitchen, no bathroom, no plumbing, no central heat or sink or stove, no wooden floors, or storm windows or window screens, no rugs or curtains, but these trivia were to be added in time to the basic felicitous house.

What it did have was a front door with a tiny entrance Porch which was enclosed within the house walls, and the chimney stack was at the back of this. The stack leaned away from the door in order to exit through the ridge of the roof. This last feature was of great importance both structurally and aesthetically.

The ladder to the loft leaned against the stack. The Hall was to the right of the door and this room was built first, facing south and east with the hearth in the northwest corner, opposite the door. Here the man and wife cooked and slept and cozied.

When children arrived they could be boosted up the ladder to the loft. As soon as possible the Parlor was added to the left of the door, utilizing the same chimney stack, thus saving materials and work and creating a central focus of warmth and cheer.

What a carrot. May such a one fall to your lot and to mine. Never was there a more sensible, cheery and comfortable house plan, easily added to and with fine circulation of air, a minimum of steps— Oh charming cottage, of thee we sing.

S   **Sash window**   **Saxon eye window**   **Saxon helm roof**

CHAPTER FIVE

The melody of our Cape Cod Cottage continues

This Cape Cod Cottage is one of the heart warmers. Built around 1815, it is typical of what was being built on the lower Cape in the first twenty-five years of the 1800s.

The landscaping includes old fashioned shrubs such as lilac, rose and wisteria. The garden in back slopes down with berry bushes to a warm hollow of apple trees. The white picket fence is just right.

An ell at the back adds much interior space without detracting from the simplicity of the facade nor adding bulk which would lessen the coziness. The windows are probably original; they have tiny hoods and they also have ears.

The ell to the left (west) is a later addition, and from the larger window we deduce that the addition has had an addition, and still later a tiny shed-roofed entry was attached. Dependencies and outbuildings that are smaller than the previous structure look natural and not forced.

The doorway has classically derived pilasters and a fanlight in the enframement and a slight hood above. The door itself is six paneled. The roof is bowed at the delicate amount of one quarter inch per foot. The color throughout is natural shingle with white trim, which is typical and which unifies the appearance of the building and blends it with its setting. (A white clapboard facade not only breaks up the quality of the total picture but is off-Cape in concept.)

The chimney, which is no longer above the front

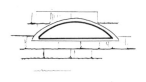

S

Segmental window   **Segmental window**   **Shed roof**

door, tells us that there have been interior changes. These changes, however, have left the original feeling in all but the arrangement of the rooms on the lower floor. The stairs that have replaced the original stairs are enclosed and steep. Upstairs are batten doors, hand-scribed beading on the vertically boarded walls and minimal window enframements. Not much of the foundation shows above ground, due in part to soil accumulations over the years.

The lists of historical architectural characteristics in the following eleven chapters reflect Cape Cod's past and also Cape Cod individuality. The characteristics are not always applicable to the present nor to off-Cape architectural history.

Historical characteristics of the Cape Cod Cottage

DEFINITIVE CHARACTERISTICS:

Asymmetry	Chimney above door
Boxy shape	Chimney rising through roof
Small, flat-topped windows	ridge
Small-paned windows	Steep roof pitch
Wood exterior	Vertical emphasis

YEARS ON CAPE COD: 1637 on

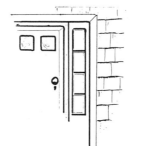

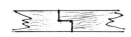

Ship lap   **Side lights**   **Sliding window**   S

GENERAL CHARACTERISTICS:

Plain walls   One and a half storeys
No ornamentation   Fanlight
Bowed roof

LANDSCAPING: Natural indigenous plantings in asymmetrical plan; evergreens, lilacs, pines; low picket fencing.

DEPENDENCIES: This mode is organic and grows naturally to the side or to the rear, each addition being of less magnitude than previous ones; also freestanding.

WINDOWS: Only the simplest, flat-topped, small-paned windows apply to this style. Window frames may extrude beyond the exterior walls by two or three inches. Sills will be simple and rather large, sometimes with ears. On facade, window pattern will be two to one side of the door or two to one side and one to the other; in the latter case the single window is generally to the west of the door. On gable end the windows may be of random placement. Decoratives are not used. Window tops may touch frieze board at eaves.

DOORS: Simple wood door, two or four or even six panels; square-topped door frame, rather coarse; simple pilasters to each side; flat-topped fanlight; bull's eyes.

ROOF: Wood, natural color; generally of steep pitch, often bowed at ¼ inch per foot; doghouse dormers.

COLOR: Older examples will be a plain color; more recent examples may be white, cream, soft yellow or gray; trim white.

TRIM: No decoratives other than regular trim board; this style is

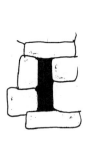

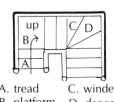

A. tread   C. winder
B. platform   D. dancer

S   **Slit window**   **Splayed window**   **Stair components**

medieval and loses character and verisimilitude if provided with fancies.

CHIMNEY: Wide, simple, no decorative courses; unfailingly directly over door and rising through ridge; brick or with pargeting over brick.

FABRIC: Unfailingly of wood, especially shingle; may be clapboard but *not* both. A building on so small a scale cannot carry two textures and tends to look as though the funding ran out after the front was done.

FOUNDATION: Low; brick; rough-dressed granite; random rubble.

L ike its English sister, the Cape Cod Cottage grew in a natural, healthy way that is a pleasure to observe. Watching the process brings us close to these people. We see their needs grow and their planning and domestic affairs develop and change to fulfill the financial, political, religious and social pattern of their lives.

At a time appropriate to the family circumstances, a room was added across the back of the house, a long room which in England was called the Outshot, but which was here known as the Keeping Room, because storage was its original purpose.

In time the Cape Cod Keeping Room became the center of most household activity. Here an oven was built into the back of the hearth. Community ovens had filled the earliest needs and this reminds us that sharing was not just a virtue but a desperate

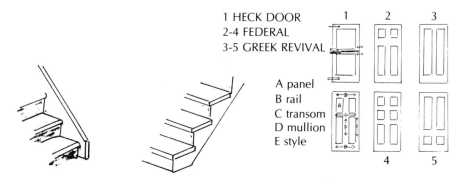

1 HECK DOOR
2-4 FEDERAL
3-5 GREEK REVIVAL

A panel
B rail
C transom
D mullion
E style

1   2   3

4   5

Stairs—closed string   **Stairs—open string**   **Style**   S necessity. When at last one's own household oven could be built, the feeling of home and domestic unity was strengthened.

The oven at the back of the fireplace requires a long hearth so that the cooking fire can be at one end and a warm but fire-free area at the other end, thus allowing access to the oven. After 1800 on Cape Cod (and fifty or so years sooner off Cape), we find that the oven gravitates naturally to the side wall. This allowed a smaller hearth to be built and gave full headroom to the baker, who no longer had to duck his head into the fireplace.

New England was deficient in the ingredients for good mortar, so stone hearths and fireplaces were seldom built until after the Revolution, but clay for brick was available here, and even mud can and has been used as mortar. Specifications for old houses on the Cape sometimes say: "And the brick shall be made from the clay in the yard."

So by Revolutionary times wooden chimneys were growing scarce. They had long been outlawed in the cities, but if you had a wooden chimney you could wait until your house burned down before you had to put up one of brick. George Washington, riding to Boston just before his inauguration, was pleased to see, on the northern part of his route, so few of the wooden chimneys which were still common in the South.

There seems to be today a misunderstanding about the term "wooden chimney." The wood was never visible but was merely the framework and this frame was heavily covered both inside and out with cob, the old form of plaster. So if you want a chimney that is reminiscent of the 1600s and the 1700s, make it of nonflamm-

T   Tongue and groove   Tracery window   Transom window

able materials and then parge it (i.e., cover it with cement).

Some of the earliest laws of our eastern cities were attempts to regulate architectural features in order to lessen fire hazards. Houses were required to have scuttles in the roof, with a ladder nearby and a bucket of water and a swab. These regulations were written with the hope that you might be able to douse a fire in your roof. Roof fires were frequent. In the cities chimneys, by law, had to be cleaned periodically (generally once a week) and the uphill fight to enforce such regulations did much to formulate early city governments.

Fire wardens were the genesis of both our police and fire departments and the fines imposed for neglect of lawful precautions against fire hazards were among our first municipal revenues.

So, you see, there is nothing new about those skylights in your roof except that they don't leak. They are not only ancient in concept but were once legal requirements of a city house, the earliest item in building codes. (Skylights are the glazed version of scuttles, also called hatches.)

The window, the skylight and the chimney are all of the same parentage, growing from a random hole in a shelter to let a bit of the inside out and a bit of the outside in, a grudging acceptance of developing needs.

In the colonial Keeping Room the fire was maintained and the Hall, which was still the principal sleeping room, was often without a fire. In time the Hall acquired a bit of privacy, that amazing new idea, then the mother of dignity but someday to be the grandmother of prudery.

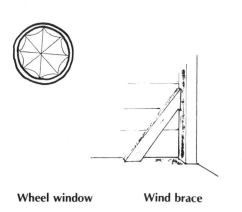

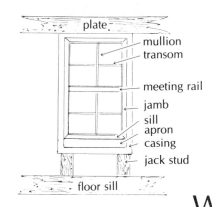

Wheel window   **Wind brace**   **Window parts**   W

The Parlor, which had been a quiet place to go and talk in the home of the English gentry, acquired after many years a specialized use here, too. First it caught all the overflow of a busy household and eventually it was a sanctorum for important events, but even into our present century it has been used as a guest bedroom.

The Cape Cod Keeping Room, reminiscent of the English Outshot whose vigor it acquired, flourished. Here was the long table. Between meals the table was used for food preparation, bread making, corn grating, the creation of pies. The room contained the baby's cradle, the spinning wheel, the quilting frame. Here of a snowy evening the master of the household would whittle spoons and other small items and make nails for the addition he would build when time permitted. By the mid 1800s he was whittling Greek Revival details, reeds and dentils, for that Grand Renovation into which fashion and a determined wife was leading him.

Here in the Keeping Room the family joined together in romps and games. Don't think that our early settlers did not romp. They were people, not cardboard cutouts from pen drawings of the late 1800s.

Here, too, was the outside door that led to the kitchen garden, to the barn (in time) and eventually to the garage. Here was established the Cape Codder's fondness for the back door, for who but a city person knocks at a Cape Codder's front door? Far in the future this backdoor primacy allowed, when plumbing entered the picture, the front door to be boarded up — on the inside only, of course. Outside it still looked just like the front door, and the old entrance porch was replaced by a modern tile bathroom. No one missed the front door because the minister no longer made regular formal calls, and at the back door there was now a Godown (later a mud room) where you could park your boots.

The Cape Codder's indifference to the importance of the front door can produce interesting results. The author once owned a Cape Cod house and the front door faced south, as it should, but any sensible city person would have considered it the back door as it was near the drive and the garage and no one used it anyway. The back of the house with its wonderful water view had what everywhere else would have been the side porch, screened to the floor, with comfortable wicker chairs and a grand breeze. The side of the house had the Godown, and also the back door with the kitchen yard and an enclosed yard for trash cans, clothes lines, the coal bin and so on. It was a wonderful house, and all traffic passed through the back door that was on the side of the house. The front door was ignored.

The Godown term came in with the clipper ships. In China this was a storage shed. (Still is.) On Cape the Godown was at the back or the side of the house and it was often down one step, which made the name especially appropriate. The Godown was sometimes made into the summer kitchen.

When space allowed, the ends of the Keeping Room were truncated for a pantry and a buttery at one end and a Borning Room at the other. The delicacy of thinking that created a Borning Room, used also for dying and other events that enjoyed this new privacy, was a growing concept in social awareness.

In medieval times all folk but the Very Great had per-formed — as did dogs, sheep and chickens — all natural functions without the restrictions of modesty or the benefit of curtains. Now we find that values were changing and an increasing ability to satisfy these new values set humans apart. In such fascinating ways does the human viewpoint alter. Philosophers may argue "better" or "worse," but "different" is hard to deny. So now we had a Borning Room; the Buttery and the Pantry we already have met in our English Hall.

A Cape Cod home, no matter how small, that has a pitched roof, has an upper area, and we cannot imagine our early settlers wasting anything. This upper area was used for general storage, which could include children.

Baskets of corn were pushed against the cool back wall, herbs were hung to dry near the mild warmth of the stack. Here, too, children could sleep. At first this area was reached by handholds on the wall such as we still find in older barns. Then a ladder was pushed against the slightly back-sloping stack.

The ladder was less precarious than the handholds were for pregnant wives and for older people. Later they were given the added comfort of flat rungs rather than roughly shaped ones, but there were still no risers.

When the stairs were enclosed within walls they were also given risers which might be of nine, ten or even twelve inches. (Our modern risers are a uniform eight inches.) Random heights for risers makes it difficult to achieve the normal rhythm that we all take for granted when going up and down stairs. But whatever the arrangement, the stairs rose sharply against the south face of the chimney stack, which itself pitched to the north. This demonstrated a perfect conjunction of necessity, ingenuity, common sense and good planning, which shows the strong thread that held together the lives of our Cape Codders and for which our admiration is unbounded.

The slope of the chimney stack allowed room for hearths — one, two or three. It also made a space into which it was possible to squeeze the stairs and it kept the stack rising through the ridge both for supportive and aesthetic reasons. Do not assume that our early settlers, driven as they were by cold, fear and loneliness had no feeling for beauty. Their eye for proportions, their instinctive awareness of good lines was as natural to them as your sensitivity to the financial and social background of your neighbors.

These Puritans and Pilgrims, living as they did on the cusp of the Middle Ages and of the Renaissance, kept the vigor of one and absorbed the perceptions of the other. We must not think that because these people were of unusual courage and remarkable physical stamina that they were not of great sensitivity and delicacy.

Thus far we have generalized and perhaps at times oversimplified fairly safely, but with the passing of time, both geographical and financial factors brought changes that must be admitted to the total picture. Each Cape town has architectural features that, while not unknown in other towns, are especially prevalent there, and the general areas have even more visible differences.

Cape Cod architecture is not a simple formula that can be expressed by the number and placement of the doors and windows of the house facade, but an intricate, three-dimensional weaving of the many factors that complicate architectural progression everywhere. Time, geography, money, knowledge, opportunity and skill ring changes and not only express local history but make intricate the dating of older houses to a fascinating degree.

The Lower Cape was domestically inclined and older houses there were smaller and more traditional. The more sophisticated form of structuring that we find on the Lower Cape often proves to have been moved there "from away."

The Upper Cape, being closer to the mainland, acquired newer ideas sooner and those houses went to two storeys more quickly. Baysiders were often more affluent than Soundsiders; they added extra rooms sooner and they "modernized" sooner, especially in the 1800s.

Cellars differ on different parts of the Cape. Provincetown cellars are sometimes aboveground (deep digging might find the water table rising to greet you). Upper Cape cellars are generally rectangular, with walls of semi-dressed granite. Lower Cape cellars were round and of brick. This is the older form and and was probably once more prevalent.

The round form was used by the clever Dutch, with whom our Pilgrims spent eleven years before coming to our shores, and it is practical to the point of brilliance. It offers no corners for mold to accumulate and it offers little hospitality to spiders and their gossamer homes. Old timers said that witches and ghosts would not stay where there were no corners to hide in.

Above all, the round cellar can be made with a minimum of

material, requiring neither massive stones nor bonding of brick. Round walls can hold back even loose sand with but a single layer of brick as the interior edges press on each other and offer increasing resistance to increased pressure.

Thomas Jefferson understood this well when he constructed his famous serpentine wall. A straight wall, besides being less amazing, would have needed bonding to stand, but the serpentine shape makes each curve add strength to the total.

All Cape cellars until modern times shared another bit of genius — the walls did not rise above shoulder height. This not only gives a shelf for storage but it encourages circulation under all of the house. Raising the walls to the floor joists inhibits circulation and causes rot that can penetrate into the floors above. A really first-class Cape cellar will either have a dirt floor or a masonry floor with dirt interstices between masonry members. Such a cellar will not need a sump pump. Cement floors are seldom successful on Cape Cod.

Room differentiation was of slow development. As homes grew in size, the Keeping Room was often changed into a kitchen; other times it became the dining room. Upper Cape homes of consequence sometimes had a harvest kitchen in the cellar. Here was a wide, outside door, a hearth, a bake oven, and an area for food preparation.

[This was long before the cellar-kitchen of the mid-1800s, which came as a city concept and assumed paid household help. From here the food rose slowly to the dining room by means of a hand-hauled dumb waiter, and you knew that dinner was coming because the dumb waiter squeaked.]

In the harvest kitchen the family gathered to butcher and preserve, amidst the sharp aroma of apple butter boiling down, the heavy scent of mincemeat and the patient clunk of the knife slicing squash for drying.

Some houses added an ell that became the summer kitchen. This summer kitchen — which was generally attached on Cape, although detached in warmer climes — was especially welcomed when stoves came into popularity to take over the job of fireplace cooking. The intense radiating heat of the stove, unlike the hearth heat which went up and out, was gladly donated by the rest of the household to be the cook's special prerogative.

Time brought changes to the house as to all things. It happened first next door — "Mary has one, John, so we must have one too." The attic was made into chambers (no New Englander ever slept in a bedroom) and the sunny house-front upstairs became two rooms, sometimes adding light and cheer through the courtesy of dormers. The back part of the attic remained storage.

The staircase then did an interesting thing. About half way up it split into two parts which ran opposite to each other and at a forty-five-degree angle to the lower run. This allowed the chamber occupants to reach their own rooms without going through the attic or through the room of the other occupant.

Upper Cape houses were often more spacious than those of the Lower Cape. Their porches had room for staircases of two or more runs, with a platform and/or with winders and dancers to make the transition between runs. This offered a new elegance of ascent and permitted newel posts and balusters that could be sawn into pretty shapes. And now we generally find risers of not more than nine inches.

Culture lag is one more item to be considered in observing older homes. While buildings in Connecticut, Rhode Island, Cape Cod, Maine and on the Islands have many relationships, many other factors make them dissimilar, and the details and time frame of one are not suitable to the other. For instance, the "exposed beams," beautifully smoothed by adze and decorated with chamfer stops, give a rich atmosphere to Connecticut buildings. These were seldom done on Cape and are not typical of our architecture before 1900.

The Cape did not achieve the sophistication of the mainland. Even the grander houses of Sandwich retain a simplicity, a restraint of interior and exterior detail that is proper to the rural and strongly traditional viewpoint of Cape Codders.

We will now ring in a change that is very important for understanding our older architecture. The floor plan that we have been delineating pertains to our medieval, that is Gothic, Cape Cod Cottage, showing how it was built and how it grew. The same floor plan pertains to some, but not all, of our next style, the Cape Cod House of Renaissance (Georgian) ancestry.

Often the Cottage grew to become the House by expanding the Parlor. Sometimes the Georgian House was built directly and the strong Cape Cod tradition of keeping that superlative floor plan with its central warmth and fine circulation continued.

But the Georgian House had its own floor plan which was very different from the traditional Gothic plan. Some folk adopted this new arrangement of rooms, especially when building a more prestigious residence. We will discuss the Georgian facade next and then its particular and individual room layout.

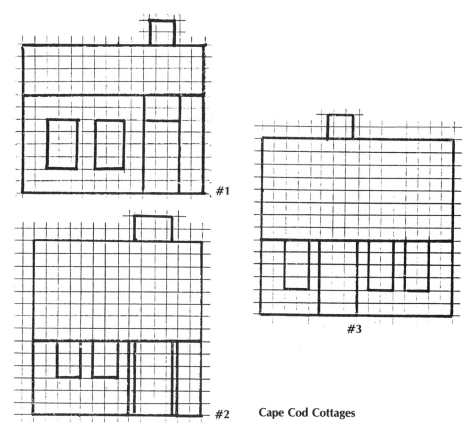

#1

#2   Cape Cod Cottages

#3

CHAPTER SIX

Georgian architecture — The story of our Cape Cod House

This is a clean-cut example of Cape Cod Georgian architecture, with its definitive characteristics unmarred by second-thought additions. The landscaping is stark, perhaps in order not to detract from the commercial application. The dependencies are to the rear and avoid the possibility of damage to the simple statement of the facade.

The windows are proper and their obvious attachment to the frieze board on the upper floor gives strength to the building's appearance. The proportions are good, with enough space given to windows to look welcoming and enough wall space remaining to look stable.

The door and side lights are fine and the semi-eliptical fanlight adds a gentling touch to the austerity of straight lines. The roof is hip and ridge, which is proper to later Georgian in this area and the color of dark red echoes the brick of more sophisticated off-Cape examples. With the clean white trim you have a dignity that is hard to match.

The chimneys are enclosed within the walls, retaining heat and making the roof line less stiff. Clapboard is a logical choice for fabric and makes the red paint feasible. The lines add horizontality, and the white trim points up the symmetrical planning. The low foundation has no doubt been lowered over the years by soil accumulation.

This simple, forthright statement of a style is always attractive, but the mode is equally handsome when done with a single storey, with or without the addition of a dormer. (A shed dormer is best, but doghouse dormers will work, too.)

Historical characteristics of Georgian architecture— the Cape Cod House

DEFINITIVE CHARACTERISTICS:

One and a half to two storeys

Bilateral symmetry

Natural fabrics

Small-paned flat-topped windows

Chimney directly above door

Chimney rising through ridge

Horizontal emphasis

YEARS ON CAPE COD: 1780 on

GENERAL CHARACTERISTICS:

Plain walls

Gabled or gambrel roof

Bowed roof

Hip and ridge roof

Low foundation

Dormers — shed or doghouse

Pilasters

Quoins

LANDSCAPING: Anything simple and indigenous; local trees, shrubs, old-fashioned flowers. Off Cape, plantings can be stiff and formal, but here asymmetry was more popular.

DEPENDENCIES: An ell to the side or back; also freestanding, but always smaller than main house.

WINDOWS: Flat headed only; decoratives never used. There may be simple flat window hoods. Windows unfailingly small paned, single or double hung. Properly, height should be twice width. Windows will be symmetrically placed on facade and also on ends of building. Window tops may or may not touch frieze board.

DOORS: Generally six panel but may be four or even two (the many-paneled doors of off-Cape houses were not used here). Fanlights, either flat headed or semi-circular; bull's eyes; side lights. There may be simple pilasters aside the door.

ROOF: Gabled, gambrel or flat; generally bowed at ¼ inch per foot, sometimes ½ inch per foot; variable pitch, natural texture. Shed or doghouse dormers. If flat, there will be a roof comb. Hip and ridge.

COLOR: Earliest examples were natural wood. May also be painted soft gray, soft yellow or soft red. Shingled roof was often painted red when walls were natural.

TRIM: On early examples, the only trim was simple pilasters at sides of door; later pilastered corner boards without cornice returns. Quoins; dentils under eaves; narrow hoods over window; enriched doorway; bull's eyes, side lights, fanlights.

CHIMNEY: Wide, plain, sometimes with a drip course; may be parged. Always directly over door and rising through ridge or at two or four symmetrical points near ends of building; seldom placed at end on Cape houses. In rare instances there was an Elizabethan grouped stack.

FABRIC: Natural wood, shingle or clapboard, but not both; both were done off Cape, and here during 1900s but not before. May be brick.

FOUNDATION: Brick; semi-dressed granite; low.

The Cape Cod House, with its balanced facade, is our expression of Georgian architecture. Here is the story of its growth and development and how it came to add graciousness and character to our landscape.

Long ago in the turbulent Roman times the Roman villa had turned its back on the world by enclosing a central courtyard from which family rooms radiated. Shops, opening onto the street, formed a protective ring around the perimeter. Compare this with the Chinese family compound to see that throughout the world similar conditions produce similar types of construction.

The medieval years in Europe were emotional times of romance and fear, of pain and faith, and of a social stability that was built on an acquiescence to an oppressive hierarchy. These conditions came in time to seethe, offering a rich and receptive environment for the Renaissance which developed in Italy and which emphasized thought above feeling.

In the 1400s the Italian Renaissance flowered among the blue and green and gold of the Tuscan hills. The architecture done at this time is the ancestor of our handsome Georgian Colonial style of house, among which are some of New England's and Cape Cod's greatest treasures.

During the early years of the Italian Renaissance there was much unrest, typical of an era of change and adjustment. The homes built at this time were not unlike fortresses and they reflected their Roman ancestry.

On the ground floor, in a central courtyard, the owner pursued his business. Picture him in his black velvet cap, belted tunic and the cape that failed to hide the knobs of his immodest knees. If he were very successful, there would be a mezzanine for storage of wares above the courtyard. (Remember that American department stores built in the early 1900s always had a mezzanine? The stores often looked like fortresses, too.)

The family rooms were on the piano nobile above the mezzanine, while servants and tenants lived on still higher storeys. Such buildings often rose to be six or seven storeys but the facades were planned to appear as though the building were of three or four storeys and the wide overhang of the roof added to the look of horizontality. This overhang provided shade to the upper parts, where the rising heat must have been overwhelming.

Vast though these buildings were, they had but one door that opened to the outside world, which is testimony to the turbulence of the times. With masonry walls they showed the placid strength of invulnerability. Designed by architects, they were horizontal in emphasis, symmetrical in plan, and handsome due to the extraordinary consideration given to achieving harmonious proportions.

A module of whole numbers was a basic tool of Renaissance architecture and this resulted in buildings that were restful and pleasing to the eye. Each component was carefully thought out both in itself and in relation to its other parts and to the total picture.

The insistence on balance sometimes gave rather static results, not allowing easily for additions or subtractions. Herein lies the limitation but also the dignity and the poise of the mode. Decoration was of classical derivation, thus being consistent with the new humanistic concern for ancient Latin and Greek civilizations.

As political tensions eased in Italy the architecture reflected the less defensive position until, in the 1500s, the great architect, Palladio, designed facades so friendly — while retaining balance, harmony, proportion and consistency — that we might live happily behind them today.

When that talented Englishman, Inigo Jones, went to Italy in the early 1600s, he thought that the work of Palladio was awesome. Returning to his native streets he did magnificent buildings that celebrated the Italian palazzi in coherence, self-sufficiency, firmness, and rectangularity, using symmetry and classical ornamentation.

This new manner of working, differing from the rambling informality of previous years, was clasped by Englishmen so warmly to their hearts that the Renaissance type of building became the standard for public construction, for homes both large and small and for cottages, and it is still both loved and done.

This method of designing we now call Georgian after the English kings who were on the throne during its developing years, and it still has the basic qualities of the Italian palazzi.

In the New England colonies there were strong ties to the mother country. If our political and financial viewpoints coincided less as we grew more independent, we still leaned on England for background and tradition in creative fields even into the late 1800s. If you question this, read your *Harper's* magazines for these years.

Living in the American colonies and on Cape were people who were proud of their new prosperity. They had survived the 1600s, which were their toughest years, and they felt established, expansive and now they reached for elegance. They wanted to live as their peers were doing in England and they wanted to show to themselves and to their immediate world that in this new life they were a permanent, decorous and affable society. As a statement of achievement the Georgian filled their requirements admirably.

Medieval architecture, arriving on Cape with our earliest settlers, was given its fullest expression here as the Cape Cod Cottage, a building that grew from a single room and that expanded organically in asymmetrical fashion. It demonstrated in England, in New England and on Cape, the vigor, lustiness and defensive determination that kept our pioneers from quitting in spite of outrageous odds.

Now the new Georgian House facade became a delicious mural with a minutely considered design that illustrated the owner's intellectual and material arrival in a world of security and growing sophistication. How warmly Cape Codders received the style, how thoughtfully they did it, and how joyfully we still view it today.

With the white gate that yields the latch so readily, the low-flowered garden, the glistening small-paned windows, the welcoming doorway and the overall sense of peace, the Georgian House sooths the heart.

Off-Cape, the Georgian interiors became set in stiff patterns and the result had a drawback. Previously the Gothic Cottages had developed around the occupants, expressing their growing domestic needs. Now the exciting new front gave an interior with a four-room grid into which people had to fit themselves. Not until the mid-1800s, when asymmetrical house plans returned to style, did houses again begin to be considered, on the interior, to accommodate individual requirements. Georgian is first of all a public statement.

In one type of Georgian interior, the tiny entrance porch with its telescoped staircase expanded to make a roomy foyer. More usual was the porch's extension in depth to become a lengthy passageway that reached the rear of the house with a second entrance doorway.

These new plans did away with the central chimney complex that had been the core of the older Cottage. The result was two

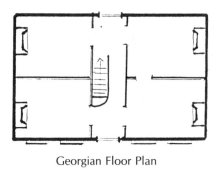

Georgian Floor Plan

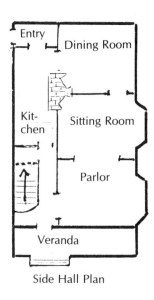

Side Hall Plan

paired or four single chimney stacks to heat the four rooms of the ground floor. In the colonial South, where the expense of heating was not a large concern, chimneys were pushed to the outer walls and these end walls were then all brick. Since enclosing the stacks lessens heat loss and adds to the comfort of a house in a chilly climate, all but the well-to-do folk here kept their chimneys inside the walls. This made for a less austere and less rigid appearance of the house, for wood looks cozier than brick, and the chimneys, pulled back from the extremities of the house, added somewhat to the gentling of the roof line.

The fenestration of the exterior was meticulously considered. Previously, windows had been openings in the wall to let in light. Now they, with the door, became the theme of the house front. Ideally the width of Georgian windows is half the windows' height, and the mullions, transoms and reveals are painted white in order to register clearly the lines and the proportions.

The glass of early English casement windows had lead enclosures called cames (pronounced "cahms"). The diamond-shaped panes were called quarries. Cames were not satisfactorily weather tight for the requirements of the new sash windows whose panes were rectangular, nor was English oak equal to the task of holding the glass.

Wood imported from Scandinavia was used but proved to be less than perfect because it did not stand up well to the ravages of time. So white lead was painted over the wood. This not only preserved the wood, but the visual aspect of clean white lines against the brick of the English Georgian was so successful that the color remains an important part of the scene. The idea of white lead to improve the staying power of wood was thus established.

The front door, later sometimes placed in a protruding bay, was in the middle of the lower storey, flanked on each side by an equal number of windows, generally two to a side, sometimes three. If there was an upper storey, each aperture there would correspond to one on the lower level.

Earliest roofs here were gabled, but the steep Gothic lines were not compatible with the new mode. The last few feet of the roof were then bent back, lowering the silhouette and yielding the gambrel roof. The idea that the gambrel was originally designed to make for more room upstairs shows itself to be false. When we look at the framing of early gambrels such as the Peter Tufts House in Medford, we see that the lower slope did not change, but only the upper slope, which hipped back. Only after the form was established did the lower slope move outward to give more head room.

Hip, and hip and ridge were also early English types and went well with the Georgian. Still later the upper angle of the roof was truncated, making a platform for a small deck which could be surrounded by a decorative roof comb. The angle at which the roof pitch changed then slid lower and lower until the Colonial Georgian can be found with a flat roof. This is pierced by two or four chimneys which are symmetrically placed, all encompassed by a decorative roof comb.

The gardens and outbuildings of Georgian houses are expected to be formal and balanced, but unself-conscious Cape Codders have always pleased themselves and were independently informal. In expressing architectural styles Cape Codders have stayed within the specific requirements of each mode while at the same time applying their personal touches. These have always enhanced the styles for local acceptance. Cape Codders have added or subtracted to make the style conform to their needs while bringing the modes into closer companionship with native colors, textures and the contours of the landscape.

Georgian was frequently done here without an upper storey, which was sometimes added later in the form of a shed dormer. Doghouse dormers were also acceptable. There was less awareness here of the historic background of the style, but a happy understanding of the beauty and fashion and a thorough ability to achieve its remarkable qualities.

England was now sending us a growing supply of excellent picture books which showed the new style and gave detailed descriptions and illustrations on how to express it, both in large and in detail. Working without benefit of architect — and, by George, he didn't need one — the Cape Cod builder, who was often the householder and who often built no more than his own domicile, had an astonishing affinity for good line and good proportions.

The Georgian mode became more than widespread. It became the signature of the Cape, the ne plus ultra of desirable homes and the basis of many spin-offs and hybrids such as the "Cape Cod Ranch."

While many older homes were built directly in the Georgian style, a careful examination of old homes and their structure will often reveal that the building was originally in the earlier, asymmetric fashion of medieval derivation. Later the proud owner brought the house up to date by extending the building until there was room for a balanced facade. We see that the Cape Cod Cottage, while often the in vitro parent of the Cape Cod Georgian House, is in reality no close relative at all.

CHAPTER SEVEN

The Georgian recipe
for your dream house

Old Cape Cod Houses are a treat to the eyes and sometimes we wonder how they got to be so. It isn't just the soft colors or the natural textures, although these two ingredients are essential, nor is it that time has put the lines slightly off true, and this does make a contribution. But there is a secret ingredient, a recondite factor that makes old houses a joy to look at. They have a sense of coziness and of home that is intriguing.

How did farmers and fisherfolk and amateur builders achieve so unfailingly an architectural charm that frequently eludes us? The answer is found in the method of designing that was used long ago. It is a simple method that has come down to us from the great architects of all the ages, and it is free to everyone. It involves the use of squared paper, and here is the story.

The beauty of Georgian has had a universal appeal above almost all styles. Only the Greek has rivaled it in ubiquitous admiration, and the reason is that both were designed with time-tested proportions, arrived at by an easy formula that produced the subtle and dependable joy that the eye and heart get from visual harmony.

The Greeks developed rules for every line, distance and level, but we have no need to follow them through such intricacies. The practical Romans simplified the Greek rules of balance and harmony and added a more worldly richness of detail to their structures.

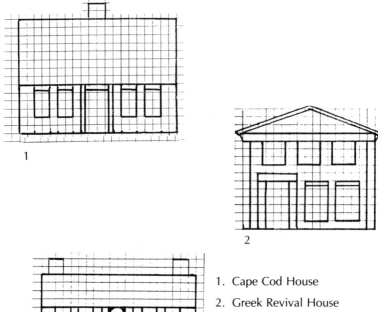

1

2

3

1. Cape Cod House
2. Greek Revival House
3. Cape Cod Federal House

The men of the Renaissance did likewise when they used the ancient civilizations as a springboard to a new aesthetic of living.

The great English architects, such as Sir Christopher Wren, further simplified and worked with the basic idea of the immense importance of proportion in design. They planned their famous structures with a module of whole numbers, a standard unit of measurement, preferably even numbers, *no* fractions. So did the great builders of the American Colonies such as Thomas Jefferson. He too worked on squared paper and so did the many unlearned men who built, with their own hands, their modest cottages. Designing on squared paper will give you good proportions, and although the method is simple, the results are thoroughly sophisticated.

There are two basic categories into which we divide all architectural styles. The first category is concerned with the directional emphasis of the building. Is it wide and low, with elements that emphasize horizontality, or is it vertical in stress, with lines running up and down that delineate height?

The second category is about the balance of elements. Is the building symmetrical, with a central feature such as a door or a veranda, or is the facade asymmetrical, with an unbalanced plan such as an uneven number of windows? To some extent those styles that are horizontal are also symmetrical and those that are asymmetrical are also vertical, but this is not a stringent rule, especially in Cape Cod examples, as we shall see.

For hundreds of years, while this country was still the undisturbed home of Native Americans, in Europe and in the British Isles, asymmetry and verticality were in vogue. This concept of structuring was symbolized by the great Gothic cathedrals whose lacy spires still excite the sky.

Such forms were organic; that is, they grew naturally to fill the owner's needs and the growth was more spontaneous than planned. This attitude reflected the era.

Small buildings, barns, and homes — all by nature more simple and smaller than churches — shared, in a necessarily limited way, the same characteristics: steep roofs, dim interiors and asymmetrical facades.

Sooner or later all things change, and the Renaissance was a major influence for change in the western world. We are talking now of those years in which Christopher Columbus was growing up, asking questions of his brother, the Map Maker, chatting with sailors and navigators and thinking about the islands that some folk said lay beyond the blue western curve of the world's edge.

Columbus, too, was affected by the new way of thinking and reasoning which resulted from an animated interest in the ancient civilizations of Greece and Rome. The new-old way of looking at life and all of its components — literature, painting, learning, worshiping, seeing — changed navigation and exploration even as it changed architecture.

The fashion for building took on classical concepts. It became low, symmetrical, reasoned rather than emotional, considered rather than spontaneous. The Renaissance building style had a boxiness of construction and a rigid balance of exterior. It was based on Greek and Roman forms, borrowing from both. It achieved a Greek simplicity of line with a Roman richness of ornamentation that was most effective.

After a hundred years or so, as we have seen, this mode reached England, and this was about the same time that the Pilgrims were setting down on our shores. Within another hundred years, but well before our Revolution, the people of the American Colonies had reached a technological and social state in which they could assimilate the new view of building.

These were years when people were still steeped in a sense of community and they built as their neighbors did, with a feeling for their role in the neighborhood and for their contribution to the total picture of their area. Around the time of our Civil War, professional architects and technical methods began to replace the old-fashioned ways, and the basic structural rhythms were lost. Squared paper was scorned.

Do you have a dream house, as most of us do? In a stolen hour we plot the crisply equipped kitchen, the dramatic bedroom with a view of the stars, and a welcoming hearth for friendly winter evenings.

We want the dream house to have an attractive facade, to present to the world as it passes the door, an appealing and thoughful face that may make people pause and say "Now THAT is a handsome house."

Squared paper is the secret. With it you can design your dream home, giving it the benefit of two thousand years of talent, knowledge and skill. Go up to the children's room or down to the stationery store and get your graph paper. You don't have to stick to Georgian or any recognized style or plan. Good proportions are appropriate to all structures. This method will give you a super barn; you can use this to set the house on the lot and lay out the garden. Just stick to the whole numbers in arranging the lines of your house, the roof, doors, windows, verandas and their relationships, and you can have a dream of a dream house.

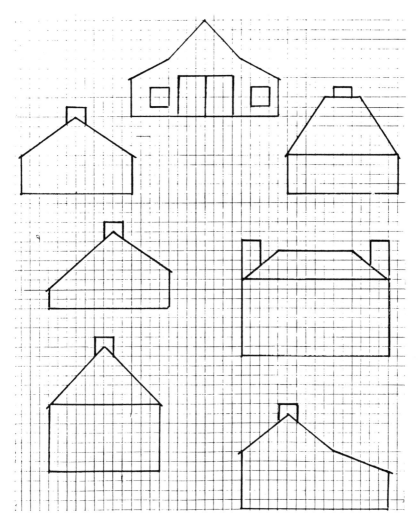

Miscellaneous squared plans

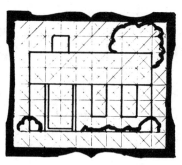

Viewing house with picture frame

The idea is of equal value if you want to use it on the inside. The great architects of the Federal style used such planning extensively.

Next, have some fun. Take an old picture frame, one with glass still in it and not too big; maybe 9 × 12 inches is a good size for you. With a magic marker, divide the glass into squares of, say, ¾ of an inch, and construct all diagonals.

Now go out and find that old house that you so admire. Hold the frame at eye level and walk toward the house until it fits visually into the frame, and you will see if the house was designed on squared paper. Success comes most often with the Georgian house that was built after the advent of the sash window, but the idea has been around a long time and was available to anyone with a bit of charcoal from the fire and a straight edge. The results were always satisfactory.

PART TWO

The styles
and their
histories

CHAPTER EIGHT

Jeffersonian Classicism and the Federal style

This handsome example of classicism is well land-scaped with trees and shrubs that enhance the picture. The outbuilding is compatible in style.

The windows are large and plain and bring down the scale of the building. Above the doorway is a roundheaded window with tracery and in the roof-pediment is an occulis with tracery. The portico columns are not overslender and the door has been brought forward with a small vestibule that is probably not original but which adds a hospitable touch. A roof rack adorns the portico.

Sophistication is given by the central bay of the facade which has been brought forward slightly; this is further defined by the based pediment in the roof. The roof itself is a simple gable, supported by deep eaves and colossal pilasters with cornice returns.

The color is soft gray with white trim, the fabric is clapboard and the foundation is low. This building is dignified and speaks to us of a day when houses were planned with a decided regard for the neighborhood, with pride in construction and with pleasure in the result.

Historical characteristics of Jeffersonian Classicism on Cape Cod

DEFINITIVE CHARACTERISTICS:
   Boxy rectangle or group of
      rectangles
   Classical trim
   Flat-topped windows
YEARS ON CAPE COD: 1815 – 1830
GENERAL CHARACTERISTICS:

Quoins	Palladian window
Columns	Semi-circular window
Pilasters	Protruding bay
Weightiness	Decorative windows
Temple front	Portico

Hip and ridge roof with
   pediment
LANDSCAPING: Semi-formal; fencing of medium height.
DEPENDENCIES: Close at rear or sides; freestanding.
WINDOWS: Flat headed; Palladian; side lights, fanlights; tracery; decorative types. Space alloted to windows may be generous, amounting to almost half of facade.
DOORS: Simpler than we will find in the Federal. Porticos with normal height columns; pilasters; pilastered corner boards without cornice returns. Veranda may have balusters.
ROOF: Gabled, with low pediment inserted at eaves; low pitch; entablature is rare; hip; hip and ridge, which may have ridge comb or roof comb.
COLOR: Pale gray, soft yellow, cream. This style is too heavy for white paint, which overemphasizes bulk. Trim may be white.
TRIM: Portico; pilasters; decorative windows; Palladian window.
CHIMNEY: Not conspicuous; simple; brick.
FABRIC: Wood, particularly clapboard.
FOUNDATION: Medium height; brick; granite.

Here is a chapter that the reader can skip but that the author may not. It concerns two styles that are no longer found frequently on the Cape but which have been influential and are still important to the overall picture.

If the reader is a serious house-peeper and he can succeed in finding examples of the two styles, he will deserve more than an amateur rating.

While the American Revolution was winding itself up, that truly versatile gentleman, Thomas Jefferson, got seriously involved with architecture. Traveling in southern Europe, he was really impressed by what he saw of Greek and Roman ruins.

In those days no one differentiated between Greek and Roman

forms except for a prestigious German art historian with the euphonious name of Johann Joachim Winklemann. He, too, was wandering around the Mediterranean and he had a shovel in his hand. Digging here and there, Winklemann declared that there was a great deal of difference between the Greek and the Roman artistic viewpoints. But scholarly news traveled in those days like cold molasses on snow, and Jefferson, as everyone else was doing, bunched Roman and Greek styles together as "classical."

Back home, Jefferson got a large quantity of squared paper and designed Monticello for himself. Working with others, he designed the state capital at Richmond, the University of Virginia and the federal capital (later burned by the British) at Washington.

Jefferson happily and successfully combined Greek columns with Roman domes and directional podiums; the result was dignified, formal and innovative with a strong classical vocabulary.

His work pleases the eye with excellent proportions and we have his plans, both elevations and floor plans, all carefully worked on squared paper.

We call Jefferson's style classicistic, to indicate that it is derivative of ancient forms, and this is an apt name. Since he was an American colonist and he created something new, albeit of known ingredients (and how can any architect do otherwise?) it seems reasonable to call this our first American style.

Jefferson's influence as a statesman, economist and president was great. His architectural influence was also widespread and his work became available in fine picture books that were then circulating. Cape Codders who were about to build substantial homes were often intrigued by these new and classical ideas and incorporated them into their houses with effective results. Classicism was a prologue to the Greek Revival whose overwhelming presence was about to make an appearance.

Since Cape Cod types are restrained in their manifestations, we have to look closely to find our examples. On Cape, this elusive style, simple but with classically derived touches, is best recognized by what it is not.

It isn't Georgian, which came before it, because the facade will not have the strong horizontal emphasis, nor need it be rigidly symmetrical. It should have a slight feeling of vertical uplift.

It won't look Federal, which came after it, because it will lack the delicacy. The window over the front door will be a solo, but it probably will not be the Palladian window, which is often Federal on Cape.

The front of the building will either be a gable or have a gable set into a hip and ridge roof. The gable should have a window of circular or semi-circular shape. There can be dentils under the eaves, pilasters on the front, and the front door might be off-center. It really should not be painted white but it probably is.

Since this mode was done on Cape from around 1800 to 1825, in the long years since then the building might have collected a Gothic veranda, a Queen Anne window and a green composition shingle roof. I'm sincerely sorry about that, for it does complicate things.

The best that we can do is offer two examples, both mid-Cape, both on Route 28 so that they can easily be found and viewed. You can study them and after that you will be on your own.

The first example is at #364 Old Harbor Road (Route 28) in Chatham. Built in 1825, before the Greek Revival came here, this house has a distinctly classical flavor. There is a low-pitched roof and the colossal (i.e., two storey) columns give a feeling of verticality. They are of very low relief and lack cornice returns or the entablature that we would find with Greek Revival. In the gable end we find a sun burst, a Roman touch.

The gable end fronts the street with three windows above and two below, but the present double door in the middle is a modern fillip and replaces a previous window. The main entrance on the south has a rectangular portico with square columns of ordinary proportions. The close growth of the many additions to the house is typical and the previous color of soft yellow was appropriate to the style. Low keyed as this house is, it is a fine example of Jeffersonian Classicism as found on the Cape.

Our second example is in Orleans on Route 28, #45. It too was once a cheerful yellow. The wonderful colors of the 1800s are being discarded again and again for somber hues.

This house is symmetrical, but with only one window to each side of the front door. The center gable has a handsome occulis window and beneath it is a round-headed window of beauty. This is directly over the portico, which has columns of normal width. The portico has been half-enclosed, at a later date than the original construction.

The colossal pilasters lack both a strong cornice return and an entablature, but they give an upward lift. The suggestion of a central bay is charming. This house has a bold richness that links it well with Jefferson's work.

The effect of this house is austere sophistication, self-confidence and propriety. The plantings shelter the house from the nearby highway. The outbuildings are inconspicuous and the ell (to the west) adds a touch of imbalance.

The windows are unadorned. The doorway, which is a Cape feature of Federal, is fully enriched and the enframement has tracery side lights, a segmental fanlight with tracery. At the side of the doorway are pilasters under an eliptical arch. The columns of the portico are not over-slender but the portico does give a sheltered, withdrawn look. The door itself is Federal six-panel. And edges are trimmed with guttae.

The roof is hip and ridge and the four chimneys are plain and properly enclosed within the walls. This suggests a four-room plan downstairs. Most of the heat of a fireplace is wasted and to put the chimney outside of the walls adds to the loss. If, however, the entire ends of the house are brick, and fires are maintained on the hearths around the clock and around the year, warmth is generated.

The facade is clapboard, the end walls are masonry, and the corner boards provide a pleasant termination to the picture. The ell is in keeping with the rest of the house; its roof is flat and the roof comb has urn-shaped finials.

The foundation is high, which adds to the air of sophistication. The gate posts have acorns and there is an elaborate pergola in the side yard that probably supports a grape vine in season.

The color of the building is pale gray-blue, with cream trim and green shutters and the result is most attractive.

Historical characteristics of the Federal style on Cape Cod

DEFINITIVE CHARACTERISTICS:

Boxy rectangle	Low roof pitch
Shadowed doorway or	Narrow windows
portico	Vertical emphasis

YEARS ON CAPE COD: 1800 – 1830 and on

GENERAL CHARACTERISTICS:

Two full storeys	Attentuated columns
Flush dormer	Hooded doorway
Plain walls	Symmetrical or
Flat roof	asymmetrical
Gable roof	Portico
Gambrel roof	Roof comb
Hipped roof	Ridge comb
Hip and ridge roof	Palladian window
Lantern	Delicacy of ornament
Broken pediment	Semi-circular fanlights

LANDSCAPING: Apt to be stiff and formal. Fencing of medium height; from this time on fencing was sized according to the size of the area of the home grounds. A flower garden at the house front would have a picket fence about eighteen inches high; a farm or estate fencing would be up to eight feet in height. The pickets were spaced for ventilation and visibility. After 1860 fencing was often solid but heights were similarly regulated. Evergreens were often used as fencing and also privet, which can be cut into arches and shapes. Random rubble (of local, not imported, stone) was frequently used.

DEPENDENCIES: Attached or freestanding; always lower than main building.

WINDOWS: Properly, these are narrow, although on Cape Georgian windows are commonly used on Federal style. Relatively little wall space is given to windows. Always small paned. Decoratives include Palladian, round headed, triangular, occulis, semi-circular. Windows on front directly above windows of lower storey, but random placement on side.

DOOR: This is a vital feature of the style on Cape. It will be enriched, but more austere than busy. The door itself will be of six panels of wood, with a semi-eliptical or semi-circular fanlight. Side lights often with tracery; columns and pilasters skinny and tall; broken pediments above door and there may be a cartouche.

ROOF: Hip; hip and ridge; gable; gambrel; flat. Generally of low pitch; may have based pediment set into roof; lantern. A flush dormer may provide a second storey.

COLOR: Soft red (to simulate brick), gray, cream, soft yellow; trim often white.

TRIM: Ovals, swags; porticos without balusters. Any restrained classical trim, such as modillions, was used.

CHIMNEY: Brick; two or four, slender, tall, near ends of building but contained within.

FABRIC: Brick; wood, shingle or clapboard.

FOUNDATION: Medium height; brick or granite.

T he next one of our two styles is easier to comprehend. With the surrender of Lord Cornwallis and the acceptance by the Colonies of our Constitution, this country disowned King George, but we have never lost our love for Georgian architecture, which continues to be built, along with its offspring, and nowhere more intensely than on Cape Cod.

The style that zoomed to the top of the Hit Parade right after the Revolution was Georgian's own child, and just as surely English in parentage and with the same Italian ancestry. The talented Adam Brothers, working in England, used a manneristic viewpoint to create something new. For the delight of their wealthy clients they fathered on the friendly and hospitable Georgian style a delicate and delightful daughter who was high spirited and also a bit neurotic. They called her the Adam style.

She was too pretty not to cross the Atlantic, and our juvenile country — like any youngster that has just found independence — took what it could from the old folks. In accepting this style we rejected the family name of Adam, and gave it a new name that was more suited to our new status — Federal.

The background of Federal, née Adam, is fascinating. Many of the great Italians whom we know as masters of the paintbrush also used their sense of line and beauty in a wider scope. Michelangelo, da Vinci, Raphael and others put their abilities to work designing buildings, many of which still stand to awe us.

The sophistication of Michelangelo's work displays what some art historians call "mannerism." A characterization of this is a gentle distortion or misuse of forms. An example is window enframements which may hold a blind window (and what is more contradictory than a blind window?), and columns, which we think of as supportive members, not originating at the ground level as they usually do, but standing above the first storey. And so on. This mannerism claimed your attention, for sure. One of Michelangelo's favorite gimmicks was to use alternating segmental and pedimented window tops on buildings, and while I haven't found this on the Cape, you will see it many places in Boston and elsewhere.

Off-Cape the terrific exponent of Federal was the amazing Mr. Bullfinch of Boston. His superb buildings have an endearing quality for New Englanders. In Salem Sam McIntire showed his genius, and the spirit of Federal was the expression of the neurotic, exciting skippers and merchants who chanced so much on tea and clipper ships, on sail and on silk, and who won and lost fortunes with the turn of the tide.

Much of Federal's beauty can lie in the interior, with oval rooms, flying staircases and delicate ceiling patterns. Although the facade has flexibility, it also has specific and definitive characteristics.

The face of Federal on Cape can be symmetrical or not. There are three storeys when the building is off-Cape, two storeys when the building is here, and this expresses again the deep and admirable respect for the landscape that Cape Codders have always had. Whether of two or three storeys, the upper level may be of dormers, especially the flush dormer. Windows should be narrower than in the Georgian, chimneys less full and roofs may be gabled, hip, hip-and-ridge, or flat with a roof comb.

The Federal doorway on Cape is what we see most often today. This is rich, shadowed, with a portico that is either square or semi-circular. There may be a cartouche over the door, with or without a broken pediment. Any columns or pilasters will be attenuated. The window over the door should be different from the others and ideally it will be Palladian.

This style, like the Classicistic, is an understated mode here and has often been lost in modernizations and additions. From old photographs and drawings we assume that we once had many more. Federal is simple to build, and it has great poise and presence.

CHAPTER NINE

The Greek Revival
as spoken here

This is a definitive Cape Cod Greek Revival house.
The landscaping is largely natural, except for some stiff
plantings around the foundation. Outbuildings are not in
view except for the ell which enhances the basic house.
Since we know absolutely nothing about this house

except what we see, let's have some fun and make a few wild guesses. It has a steeply pitched roof and no entablature, so it may not have been built directly in the style but may have been an older house. Then it probably once faced south and was given a quarter turn in order to front the street and to provide a gable end as a foundation for the new Greek Revival facade.

This all might have happened around 1850 – 1860. East is to the viewer's left, and the present front door faces north, roughly. The east wing was then added and also a veranda with fine Doric columns (Doric has a plain capital and no base). The ell roof pitch appears less steep than that of the main building.

The windows, with their long rectangular lights, were added, and the window hoods might have been added or they might well have been original because they fit either qualification. The door enframement, with its splendid pilasters and handsome lintel, appears to have been an amendment to the facade, but this does not detract from its beauty.

Glory of glories, there is a wooden storm door and wooden storm windows. Furthermore the shutters work, they fit the windows and the lower louvers are adjustable. Another wonderful consistency must be credited to the owner, for all of the windows — old section, new section, attic and dormers — although of differing sizes, have been treated the same, with the same number of panes and similar muntins. (On a window the crossbars are transoms, the vertical bars are mullions, and they both qualify as muntins.) And except under the veranda, they have similar hoods. (I can get equally thrilled when every window in a house differs.)

If our basic assumption is correct, pilastered corner boards with cornice returns were added, the large chimney removed and the small, stove chimney added. The fabric is wood clapboard, the color white with black trim and the foundation is low. This house is a treasure and its upkeep is superlative.

Historical characteristics of the Greek Revival on Cape Cod

DEFINITIVE CHARACTERISTICS:

Basic temple form	Cornice returns
Trabeated doorway	Small window lights
Pilastered corner boards	White paint

TIME ON CAPE COD: 1830 – 1875

GENERAL CHARACTERISTICS:

Entablature	Plain walls
Narrow chimney	Symmetry
Gabled roof	Columns
Low roof pitch	Veranda
Based pediments	Tall front windows
Door lights	Flat-headed windows
Frieze	Portico
Asymmetry	One and a half to two full
Window hoods	storeys
Horizontality	

LANDSCAPING: This varied greatly. Cape Codders did very little planting close to the building, because plantings hold moisture. Scattered trees, evergreens. White paint asks for the softening influence of plantings. Moderately ornate fencing painted white; live green fencing.

DEPENDENCIES: Off Cape Greek Revival was generally symmetrical, but on Cape symmetry was often ignored and without prejudice. Dependencies, if attached, are well back from house facade; more often they are freestanding.

WINDOWS: Flat-headed windows with small lights (i.e., panes). On front the windows are long, almost the height of interior rooms. They will be symmetrically placed on facade, but random on sides. Ribbon windows under eaves; occulis or other simple decorative in gable end. Windows may have slight hood, either straight or pedimented.

DOORS: Traditional Greek Revival doors on Cape are of two lengthy panels or two short panels at bottom of door and two others going to the top. Front door may have two, four or six panels. Door framing is trabeated without exception, with a straight lintel and pilasters or columns which are usually Doric, occasionally Ionic. Side lights, straight-headed fanlights. Steps down from front door are simple and low.

ROOF: This is a gable roof of low pitch if scratch-built. If an older house has been brought up to fashion, the pitch will pertain to the original house. Often bowed at ¼ inch per foot. Dormers of all kinds can be found, but the doghouse dormer most usual. Pediments in gable may have a base.

COLOR: This is the only style of the 1800s that can be white without explanation. Soft gray, tan, cream or light soft yellow not unknown, although these colors often followed the original white. Shutters were often omitted from Greek Revival or removed when an older house was brought up to fashion, but they were sometimes gray, green, white or black. Conspicuous colors are unfortunate as they detract from the appearance of the house. Gothic was sometimes overlaid on Greek Revival, resulting in some color confusion. Greek Revival churches in the late 1800s were often gray or tan, but probably they were originally white and given the pigmentation when white went out of fashion.

TRIM: Pilastered corner boards; entablature; columns either round, engaged or pilastered, fluted or plain; pillars; the rich post and lintel door enframement; wide verandas without balusters. For small decorations the anthemion, acanthus and frets were used.

CHIMNEY: As inconspicuous as possible; narrow; brick with a drip course; placed behind the roof as far as possible.

FABRIC: Greek Revival on Cape Cod was of wood, generally clapboard; if shingles are present, they are probably not original.

FOUNDATION: Almost always brick; medium height.

Greek Revival is the most usual form of older architecture on Cape Cod today. The buildings of the 1600s and of the 1700s that we know as the Cape Cod Cottage and the Cape Cod House have become far less numerous than they once were.

Many of the earliest of our old buildings were lost to fire due to thatch roofs or poor chimney mortar, and damp rot took others; some were absorbed, as finances permitted, into newer, larger structures; others were disassembled, such wood as was still good being saved for reuse. No Cape Codder worthy of the title would throw away anything that could be used again.

Cellars and attics are the most revealing, story-telling parts of a house. Go down into the cellar of an older house and look up at the joists of the floor above you. You may see old mortise cuts, patterns of handmade nails, groupings of machine-cut nails —all of which suggest that this wood has been used in two or three previous structures. There is nothing new about recycling here.

Greek Revival was popular on Cape between 1830 and 1875. In those days dimension timber—trees felled and cut into sized lumber before shipping—was readily available, arriving as deck cargo on schooners from Maine, Nova Scotia and the New Bedford area.

A burst of prosperity from salt works and then from cranberry bogs helped finances on Cape, and labor was not expensive. Besides, as Seth said one night at the supper table, "For heaven's sake, Hitty, I can build a house. Built our barn, didn't I? Dem fine barn. Cows love it. Well, 'course I know you aren't a cow, Hitty —" and so on until the fireflies sparkled in the yard, and Seth built the house.

Never has there been a more glorious tribute to the aesthetic sensitivity and the ability of Cape Codders, indeed of all New Englanders. Never have so many amateur carpenters created — built is an inadequate term here — such lasting beauty with such truly happy results as was done in the forty-five years of the Greek Revival on Cape Cod.

Often working with squared paper for basics, often still including the delicate and traditional camber of the bowed roof, using one of the many plan books then available, Seth and his friends made domestic gems.

I, and maybe you too, love the Greek Revival, but it had its detractors. Some folk said that it was ridiculous to see a woman in hoop skirts or a man in a frock coat issuing from a Greek temple. Others decried the use of white paint. They said that large quantities of white paint jarred the eye and that buildings properly should blend into their surroundings. These were good points, but nothing could hold back the tide of the Greek Revival.

People were enthusiastic about using this form for schools, churches, colleges, town halls, farmhouses, and homes by the hundreds on Cape and by the thousands off Cape. Early Greek temples had been wood before they were stone and marble, so translating back into wood was no problem, but temples had never had window glass, wood stoves, or plumbing. Temples had never had chimneys, kitchen ells, lace curtains, what-nots covered with shells from Madagascar, or a veranda with rocking chairs. That the buildings now assimilated these amenities expressed great determination on the part of the builders and much flexibility on the part of the building. Why, some folk even had templed outhouses in the back yard. That the result was triumph after triumph is astounding.

The source of the interest in this fashion was many-faceted. Much of the impetus came from the appearance, from the simplicity and restful horizontality of the lines. Without this basic charm the style never could have stood up to its inherent problems.

We know that the Renaissance had sparked a renewed interest in the classical world. An educated man was supposed to have a knowledge of architecture and at least a smattering of Latin and Greek, enough to quote Horace when he wanted to impress someone. "Tibi splendet focus" a man might carve on his chimney breast — "For you the hearth fire burns."

Quite a few towns on Cape Cod struggled to maintain an Academy. These were private schools whose primary thrust was to teach Latin and Greek. While the exigencies of earning a living held many a boy to the deck of his father's schooner or out in the turnip field, those who could do so went to the Academy to learn "the tongues," as Latin and Greek were then called.

With the advent of the 1800s, the world had began to heat up for revolution and democracy. The tumultuous changes that altered the financial and social structure and the living and thinking patterns of occidental man are what we call the Industrial Revolution.

In 1776 those uppity American colonies revolted; in 1789 the French bourgeoisie followed suit. In 1821, Greece tried to shake off the shackles of the Turks, and when the western world learned of the massacre at Chios and the bloody defense of Missolonghi, a strong current of feeling followed Greece's fortunes.

Ladies responded by wearing fillets in their hair and by reclining on couches that were open at one end. Before they went out in the evening, fashionable women poured water over themselves so that their gown would cling and they would look, they hoped, like statuary. (I can't guarantee that this was done on Cape.)

New viewpoints call for a compatible architectural expression.

For all of the upheaval brought about by the new technologies of production, new concepts of earning one's bread, and a change of emphasis from agrarian to urban living, this was still a traditional society.

In finding architectural affirmation, the burgeoning middle class sought, in the building forms of Greece, a stable tradition of democracy and culture. Culture has always been the tertiary goal of people whose primary aims are financial and social betterment.

We were as yet unaware of the technical refinements of Grecian architecture and this was probably just as well, because the knowledge might have confused us. We did appreciate the resulting appearance of strength, lucidity and beauty, and we wished to ally ourselves with the Grecian spirit as we understood it.

The Grecian temple, resting on a grassy hillside, is considered to be among the most sublime results of man's creativity. Our eyes are pleased by the surety and the tranquility of the lines and the excellent balance of proportions. When clouds pass across the sun, the light, weaving in and about the columns, shows the richness so subtly developed by the articulation of the facade. It all looks perfect to the eyes — but it was not achieved by happenstance.

The Greeks brought to building not only a technical skill that amazes us but a consideration for aesthetic detail that may be unequalled in history. The basic solution to engineering problems that involve mass and weight must have been slave labor and unending patience. More astonishing is the interest, mathematics and time that they put into specifics in compensating for the visual quirks that pertain to matter when it is surrounded by space.

That which we see is the product of the circumstances under which we see it. The color, direction, amount of light, neighboring objects, distance and the conditioning of our own background control every observation that we make.

The distant hills are not truly lavender, but the same green as the grass upon which we stand. The rising moon is not larger at the horizon than it will be at the zenith. We consider as childish in concept a picture that shows railroad tracks running parallel from the front to the back of the canvas, with the train upon them as large at the far end as it is at the near end. Yet we know that railroad tracks do not converge in the distance and that the train and its passengers are not actually shrinking as they move away from us.

The European man looks in front of him, for there lies his interest, but the aborigine looks at his periphery, for there may lie his dinner or his enemy. Many art forms — and architecture when it rises to art — are based upon the correction, confirmation or distortion of our visual illusions.

Old-style Greek temples, such as the temple of Poseidon at Paestum, are ponderous. Their columns push against the ground and the building is oppressed by the weight of the entablature and the pediment. Later types such as the Parthenon give a feeling of upward lift and the entablature rests lightly and stabilizes the whole.

The differences were achieved in large measure by learning to understand and compensate for a number of optical illusions. For an example, we know that two parallel lines seem to bend toward each other at midpoint. Therefore on later temples the stylobate — the massive platform on which a temple sits — will be four or five inches fatter at the middle than at the ends. All this, my friends, on a stretch of marble a hundred feet long.

In like manner the great columns that are made of weighty drums, each of which was turned and smoothed until the fit was perfect, swell slightly amidships, but only a few inches in forty feet of height. Lest columns against the sky appear thinner than the other columns that show against the building, corner columns are slightly thicker and closer to their fellows than the other columns in a row.

To lessen the impression that the building is leaning over the beholder as he looks up, its vertical lines will all incline toward the center so that if continued upward, all lines might eventually meet at a single point. Even lettering over door frames was adjusted to be faintly wider at the top so as not to give the appearance of being narrower when viewed from ground level.

All of these disciplines had to mesh and be apparent only in effect, and these and similar refinements have helped Grecian building to hold the admiration of the artistic and the lay world for two thousand years.

In adapting the temple form to the needs of life in the 1800s, flexibility was achieved by using certain Roman forms such as the round Roman arch, the dome, the podium with its directional emphasis, and the versatile brick. There were also modifications that were not of classical derivation, such as steeples for churches.

Our Cape Cod friend, Seth, when he built that house for Hitty, built directly in the style. The house was of two storeys and the roof pitch was low. The chimney was narrow and inconspicuously placed near the back of the house. This told discerning neighbors that Hitty had one of those great black stoves to serve up the heat and that the fireplace now had a permanent display of dried grasses.

There was a slight entablature running around at eave level and low pediments over the windows. The door was post and lintel, and Seth made it just a bit fancier than that of his neighbor to the south by using Ionic capitals on the pilasters at the door. There were glass lights running around three sides of the door and the lights were rectangular.

At the corners of the house were low relief pilasters and the colonnade framed a side veranda where Hitty could sit to shell peas of a summer's afternoon.

Seth's neighbor to the north had a really old cottage. Determined to be in style, the cottage was given a quarter turn, which was no great problem in those days, so that the end of the house now fronted the street instead of facing south as it had previously. The shutters were removed and so was the great chimney stack. A skinny new chimney now crouched behind the roof line.

The new front offered a basic temple silhouette, and the door was placed there and given the post and lintel enframement. With pilastered corner boards and cornice returns and two coats of white paint, this house was handsome. Now three Greek Revivals sat in a row; within two more years there were five of them.

Inside the house Hitty had a double doorway between the two front rooms. There were pediments over the door frames and over the windows, and the front windows reached almost from the floor to the ceiling.

Cape Cod Greek Revival has always had a happy freedom of its own. Often minimal in its statement, it is more relaxed, less self-conscious than off-Cape, architect-designed buildings. And it is almost unfailingly handsome.

Hitty's children and grandchildren cherished her home as she had, but her great-grandchildren sold it and it was "condo-ized." With a lack of appreciative understanding on the part of the new owners, the characteristic qualities were lost, and the loss of the whole was greater than the loss of its parts.

CHAPTER TEN

Gingerbread and Railroad —
The Gothic Revivals
on Cape Cod

The storybook quality of Gothic Revival is clear here. The depth and accent of shadows add greatly to the drama. The windows are the two-over-two sash that was so popular. They have small hoods and tiny labels. Labels were devised to keep rain off the window glass of stone buildings, but these are more decorative than utilitarian.

The two bays add interest to the facade and light and pleasure to the interior. The doorway between them acquires mystery through the shadows in which it is immersed. This house is close to the main road, and in past times it must have been delightful during summer evenings to sit and rock and watch the neighbors stroll by.

We see the steep roof and the exhilarating swoops of the gables; the shadows that result add pattern and dimension. The richest shadows of all are the creation of the lacy barge boards of two-dimensional scroll work. These shadows grow and shrink with the passage of the sun, and we regret the scarcity of such pleasant frivolities today.

The chimneys are plain, the fabric is clapboard, and the foundation is low. The previous fabric of this building was shingle, with diamond-shaped shingle inserts. The strong upright of the veranda pillars, the flat of the veranda roof, and then the verticality of the gables makes a dynamic composition. This building is an asset to its town and deserves respect and appreciation.

Historical characteristics of the first Gothic Revival on Cape Cod — Carpenter's Gothic

DEFINITIVE CHARACTERISTICS:

Steep roof	Soft, earthy paint colors
Asymmetry	2D decorative trim
Vertical emphasis	Brackets
Narrow windows with large lights	

YEARS ON CAPE COD: 1830–1880 and on

GENERAL CHARACTERISTICS:

Articulated silhouettes	Triangular windows
Corner veranda	Tower
Gablets	Tracery windows
Dormers	Buttresses (on churches)
Oriels	Gingerbread
Door hoods	Barge boards
Ancones	Labels
Grouped windows	Weathering surfaces (on
Balcony	churches)
Gothic arch	Steep gables

LANDSCAPING: Indigenous plantings asymmetrically placed; exotics such as might be brought home by sea captain. Fences were now sometimes painted to match trim of house; generally of wood; some were one-of-a-kind and quite ornate; sizes remained adjusted to area.

WINDOWS: Flat topped in groups of two, three, four; long and narrow with three or four lights only; angular rather than rounded.

DEPENDENCIES: Freestanding or attached, but less massive than main building. A home-farm complex might have a long line of buildings and the barn at the end might dwarf the house.

DOORS: Plain four-paneled. Might have glass inserts of plain or colored glass. Panels might be vertical or horizontal. Door frame simple, but hood and ancones rich (but always 2D).

ROOF: Steep, with steep gables; steep dormers; 2D barge boards of repetitive pattern; brackets.

COLOR: Color is mandatory with this style, with the exception of Gothic being overlaid on Greek Revival (not really a good idea). Two close rich earth colors or two shades of the same color. Colors tend to be heavy. White not used except as accent — i.e., yellow walls, red window surrounds and white muntins.

TRIM: It was not uncommon for Cape Codders to lay Gothic over

Greek Revival, particularly in regard to verandas that might be added. When they did this, the color was often white, with brackets, veranda balusters and a triangular window in the gable end. On the uncomplicated Gothic there would be two-dimensional scroll work (never turned work); brackets, barge boards (also called verge boards), labels, balusters; roof comb; diapered shingles; lanterns (also called cupolas, belvederes, widow's walks); towers; turrets.

CHIMNEY: Narrow, indicating no flu liner; tall; sometimes cater-cornered to ridge; always brick; decorative courses.

FABRIC: Wood; shingle or clapboard, never both.

FOUNDATION: High, brick, with decorative shadow courses.

Once there was a boy whose hair was wayward in all directions, but his brown eyes looked clearly at you without flinching. This boy was as sharp and bright as a package of new needles. In the home, in the field and in the neighborhood, this boy's mind sparkled, and the neighbors shook their heads. No good came of being smarter than the other boys. "They" said that young Suger had taught himself to read, and that must be devil's handiwork.

Poor, kind, busy providing for a numerous family, his parents took his warm young hand one day and walked up the hill to the Monastery and gave him to Mother Church. This was in the year 1091 and the gift, gladly given, graciously received, blossomed into happiness for all concerned.

In their old age, Papa and Mama Suger always had bread in the pantry. When the boy had become a man, Mother Church grew in power and prestige through his wisdom and determination. Suger was companion to kings: to Louis VI, called "The Fat", and to Louis VII, called "The Young" (he was the one who married the incredible Eleanor of Acquitaine). Suger became Archbishop of his country, France, and was Regent when his king went on the Second Crusade in 1147.

No one could call Suger a modest man. He was a persistent name-dropper — his name — which he inscribed wherever possible on his Abbey Church of St. Denis. His self-confidence and ambition were vast, as was his power. His political impact on France continued long after his lifetime, and his influence on architecture is still a force.

Indeed, on a curve of sand that had been carelessly flicked off by a glacier, that long arm into the ocean that we call Cape Cod, and which in Suger's day was still four hundred years from being "discovered," the Gothic style with which Suger is credited is still important.

But back in the year 1136, the Abbey Church of St. Denis on the Ile de France was already four hundred years old and the building needed drastic help. Old and tired, it pressed against the earth with the obdurate sulkiness of early Romanesque architecture. Suger and his workmen, in rebuilding St. Denis, took known ingredients and combined them into a new way of thinking about structure.

Suger and his men combined the pointed arch, which allows far greater height than can ever be achieved by the round Roman arch; the flying buttress, which supports walls so that their unseeing bulk can be replaced by scintillating glass; and the ribbed vault, which gives us the breath-stopping, upward-reaching interiors of Gothic cathedrals; and they had a new recipe for beauty.

Those who saw this new assemblage of ideas looked with wonder and told those who had not yet seen. The word spread that Gothic was awesome.

We have no trouble accepting Gothic as a style when we see it in the energetic masonry music of great churches. We recognize the transcendent verticality, the dim interiors with the softly moving magic of stained glass and the rhythmical planning of the components.

But Gothic, when condensed into smaller buildings, has less of the mode to identify it. When we see a small cottage with a steep roof and a single narrow window next to the door, we must consider carefully, if we are to understand the relationship between cottage and cathedral. There is the interior quality, and the strong feeling of life and growth and movement that they share as part of their medieval background.

Our Cape Cod Cottage, with its steep roof, off-center doorway, off-center chimney and the small windows that give you a sense of containment and protection when you are inside, is of this background and family.

Gothic waned as a force in fashion, and the boxy rectangularity of the Georgian and Greek Revival ruled. And then one day the western world had had enough of pressing its nose against reality, and a romantic movement sat up, looked around, stretched and knew that its day had come.

The romantic movement gave us the writings of Poe, of Goethe and Sir Walter Scott; the poetry of Keats and Wordsworth, and the Hudson River School of art. All of this embellished the new feast of sentiment.

Those were halcyon days, when childhood was said to be all delight, and boys and girls walked hand in hand through fields of flowers that never wilted or went to seed. Ladies did not have legs, although they were allowed to have limbs, and babies were found, fully clothed, under sufficiently large heads of cabbage.

Entire Gothic novels were written in which no mention was made of eating, shopping, cooking, or cleaning house. We assume that even humble homes had a backstage crew who set the props each morning and cleared the stage each night for a cast who never got dirty, never ate or performed any other bodily functions. And all stories stopped when the hero and heroine got married, for of course They Lived Happily Ever After.

In England Gothic had remained a part of the visible landscape in castles, churches, homes and cottages that had been built to last for hundreds of years. The appropriate architecture for this new romantic viewpoint was Gothic, the architecture of the Age of Chivalry, of the Perfect Gentil Knight and his beloved Lady who was always adored but never rumpled.

English architects were quick to contrive wedding-cake houses to fit in with the new-old way of thinking. America now had architects of her own, both imported from abroad (Calvert Vaux) and natives of great talent (Alexander Jackson Davis and Andrew Jackson Downing). These men published books filled with intriguing pictures of cottages and mansions. The texts of these books were very readable and also were filled with practical information.

The new mode was picturesque, exciting, different and easily achieved, and it came to Cape Cod around 1835. We called it Gingerbread Gothic or Carpenter's Gothic because of the lacy, two-dimensional trim that skipped along the eaves and at the top edge of the veranda. There were also delightful brackets wherever there was an angle to accept them.

Any simple house could be brought into style with a few bundles of these wooden whimsies plus a coat of warm-colored paint and contrasting trim color. Many were, and this gracious accommodation added to the popularity of the style.

Splendid houses were built in the mode. Winfred, Hitty's cousin, built the most elegant of all, with a tower, a balcony, and an oriel in the front room. The oriel had five windows in it, and each window had four lights, two up and two down.

A hundred and thirty years later the house had lost its tower and its balcony to the weather and to problems of upkeep, and only the oriel remained to tell of the house's former illustrious appearance.

Staying in first place in a beauty contest is never easy. The Greek Revival and the Gothic were both popular at the same places and at about the same time. While beaming on their audience, they each elbowed the other in furious jealousy.

Suddenly two new styles, both of Italian origin, danced up onto the stage. For a brief time they were wildly acclaimed and Gothic left the stage in a huff.

Gothic returned shortly, having changed her frilly costume for one of greater boldness, and again this old girl, beautiful and vibrant after seven centuries, took first place. Her new costume had come by railroad from Philadelphia and had been designed by that brilliant architect, Frank Furness.

In less symbolic language, Greek held her own, but Gothic waned. In Philadelphia, Frank Furness thought that there was still much vitality in Gothic. From his drafting table came a new version of Gothic that kept the verticality, the asymmetry, the thin windows and the pointed arches and towers. But the light touch of gingerbread was put aside and a coarser, more structural trim was used. The mandatory soft colors remained.

This cheerful style was perfect for railroad stations. Colorful, and sturdy in appearance, the decorations were more easily maintained than the delicate gingerbread of the earlier Gothic revival.

The narrow, four-paned windows are typical of the mid 1800s; the door is practical, and the commodious roof could be extended to provide shelter for passengers. In this example the passengers could wait inside in poor weather, with warmth from the pot-bellied stove and a good view of the town with its school and churches.

The tower, with its candle snuffer roof, is a fine balance to the boxy building and adds the bit of drama that is very welcome. The color is soft yellow with soft red trim. The fabric on the lower portion is clapboard. The change of surface on the upper half with the belt course and the trim line, lowers the scale of a rather tall building.

The foundation is low and the landscaping minimal. One hundred years have not diminished the staunchness of this building.

Historical characteristics of the second Gothic Revival on Cape Cod — Railroad Gothic

DEFINITIVE CHARACTERISTICS:

Asymmetrical plan	Narrow windows with large
Vertical emphasis	lights
Steep roof	Bi-coloration
Coarse decorations	

YEARS ON CAPE COD: 1860 – 1890 and on

GENERAL CHARACTERISTICS:

Articulated silhouette	Triangular windows
Corner veranda	Eave brackets

<table>
<tr><td>Tower</td><td>Gothic arch</td></tr>
<tr><td>Turret</td><td>Decorative windows</td></tr>
<tr><td>Gablet</td><td>Grouped windows</td></tr>
<tr><td>Dormers</td><td>Tracery</td></tr>
<tr><td>Balcony</td><td>Heavy bracing</td></tr>
<tr><td>Oriels</td><td></td></tr>
</table>

LANDSCAPING: Asymmetrical plantings, same as First Gothic.

DEPENDENCIES: Ells to side or rear. On farm complexes contig-uous buildings might form a J or L shape. Freestanding. Barns on occasion would dwarf the main house.

WINDOWS: Many decorative shapes and variations on Gothic arch; grouped windows; oriels; bays.

DOORS: Generally four panels, often with single large light in upper half; door hood with ancones; high stoop.

ROOF: Multiple roofs, all steep. Steep gables; tower; turret. Wood, slate or composition shingles; shingles often of several colors arranged in patterns.

COLOR: Bi-color or poly-color; heavy earth colors of red, orange, yellow, tan or brown, with contrasting trim color or close shade of same color. White not used except as emphasis. Roof color may be red, green, natural, black or gray.

TRIM: Brackets; diapered shingles; turned balusters; ridge combs; coarse bracings. See characteristics listed above.

CHIMNEY: Brick; narrow; multiple; with decorative courses.

FABRIC: Wood, either shingle or clapboard, but never both.

FOUNDATION: High; brick; decorative shadow courses.

This Second Gothic Revival is often called Railroad Gothic, for those were the days when the Union Pacific Railway and the Central Pacific Railroad had met (1869). In a tailcoat and top hat ceremony, a golden spike was driven to join together the tracks laid by the two companies, and transcontinental service across the United States was established.

Within a few years forty thousand railroad stations were built, some with convenient railroad hotels next door. Many stations were built in this dramatic and colorful new version of Gothic to awe the customer and advertise business. The Second Gothic Revival was simple, cheery and effective.

The Railroad came to Cape Cod and made life here quite different. Cape Codders could now visit the city for business and pleasure after a short, relaxing ride. City dwellers found it easy to visit the Cape. In those days folks often came for the summer, and the train trip was now part of the fun. Many folk who could not stay the whole summer found an easy way to stay for two weeks.

The train also conveyed to the city, rapidly and inexpensively, the products that previously had been shipped by truck. Turnips, strawberries, asparagus and fish now zipped along the way. So did sons and daughters of wage-earning years. Financial returns from these ventures were sent back in the mail train.

A major impact of Second Gothic Revival on Cape Cod and the Islands came from the building of the Camp Meeting Grounds at Oak Bluffs, Eastham, Wellfleet, Harwich, Yarmouth, Craigville, and so forth.

The wonderful story of Camp Meetings starts in 1799 when a youth, Lorenzo Dow of Connecticut, went to an early meeting in Kentucky and got revival fever.

Camp Meetings were the hub of religious and social life in the rural South. Homes were too far apart for people to attend church so it became the custom for the church, in the form of the minister and his horse, to attend the people.

These ministers were circuit riders who touched each locality once a year, and from all the surrounding farms and hamlets people gathered for this annual happening. Here, in tents, covered wagons and blankets-under-the-stars, folk spent a week of prayer, socializing, and singing. Elderly ladies exchanged gossip, women exchanged recipes and complaints, young people met, dogs swapped bites, men swapped horses and couples got married and baptized the baby in a single ceremony.

Young couples couldn't always wait, and the haying wouldn't wait for a three-day ride into town to get married, but everyone knew that things would be made "alright" as soon as the circuit rider came.

The preacher — sometimes one, sometimes several, sometimes as many as a hundred — with an enraptured audience, had a rich sense of importance and mission. Lorenzo Dow wanted some part of this exhilarating action, and he became a circuit rider of passion, drive and fame. His fervor as an evangelist did much to bring the Camp Meeting idea to New England, where it was warmly received.

While not having the desperate social need of the remote southern farmers, New Englanders were as gregarious as anyone, and here was an opportunity par excellence to have a first-class party under religious auspices.

And where shall we go for a vacation? Why, to Cape Cod of course. The first Camp Meeting on Cape was at South Wellfleet, followed by one at Eastham. Getting ashore on the bay side from the Boston boat, which was a side-wheeler, was made difficult by the sand flats. When the tide was out, no one could get in. So when the railroad was established, the enterprise moved to South Yarmouth.

At first people stayed in tents, but this informality presented problems, so small cottages were built. The Second Gothic Revival was in full force, having arrived via the many popular periodicals then available. This became the dominant style, giving character, color and zip to the Camp Meeting Grounds.

Oak Bluffs is the most famous of these religious gathering places. Asbury Park, New Jersey, and Ogunquit, Maine, both started off as Camp Meeting Grounds. On Cape Cod, Yarmouth and Craigville hold the honors. Scattered through the Cape you will find little cottages that have broken loose from their ecclesiastical moorings and become individual vacation homes.

Churches have always had a good relationship with the Gothic mode. After all, that's where it started. On Cape Cod there are many splendid examples of the pointed style, presents to us from the good Archbishop Suger. The churches are not always of stone; sometimes they are of shingle, with shingle-clad buttresses. Sometimes they are symmetrical, perhaps mildly diluted by Greek Revival features, but still basically Gothic in detail and in vertical emphasis.

We find Gothic style houses still being built today for private homes. Some people want a rather dramatic, Colonial exterior, and a feeling of my-home-is-my-castle when they are inside. Gothic does this exceptionally well.

Many of the condo-groupings have a distinctly Gothic flavor. They are defensive, strongly communal, with typical soft coloration, highly articulated silhouettes, and a withdrawn, upreaching air. These clusters remind us of the Middle Ages when people, lusty in the pursuit of their pleasures, were wary of the outside world and shared homes and groups of homes where they felt anonymous and protected.

Here we see again how responsive architecture is to every phase of our political and social life. The chip-on-the-shoulder individualism of the 1950s – 1970s, when Tudor cottages and Swiss chalets sat side by side, when pseudo-antiques and modern types lived in close proximity, has gone.

Now a worried world seeks protective housing, congregate dwellings with a guard at the gate and amenities within. In community we seek strength and a sense of belonging.

CHAPTER ELEVEN

Two fine Italian hands — The Italian Villa and the Tuscan Villa

This Italian Villa has the requisite characteristics for its mode. The building is asymmetrical, it is tall and has a tower that adds verticality. The landscaping is natural, with trees that soften the angularity of the style. The dependencies and outbuildings are inconspicuous.

The windows are long and narrow and have the large lights that people were proud to display during this era. There is a triangular window in the tower.

The roof is well articulated, with a helm roof in the tower and a Jerkin Head on the main roof. The overhangs, which have brackets of unusual elaboration, add horizontal emphasis that keeps the building from seeming too high.

Other trim is two-dimensional sawn work that is both delicate and ornate, and its horizontal stress helps to balance the building with its strong upward-reaching gable end and colossal pilasters.

The color is soft tan, the trim white and the foundation of medium height.

The building is dramatic and picturesque, with an opulence of shadows that is balanced by the plain wall material. Relatively simple to build, although no longer easy to maintain, the movement of this facade and the flow of its silhouette show us why this style was once so popular.

Historical characteristics of the Italian Villa style on Cape Cod

DEFINITIVE CHARACTERISTICS:

Asymmetry	Large window lights
Vertical stress	Group of boxy rectangles
Tower	Bi-coloration
Plain walls	

YEARS ON CAPE COD: 1850 – 1870 and on

GENERAL CHARACTERISTICS:

Occulis window	Round-headed windows

High foundation   Semi-circular windows
Mutules   Classical trim
Ornate chimney   Deep shadows
Entablature   Dentils
Columns   Labels
Balcony   Pilasters
Veranda   Brackets
Based pediment   Grouped windows
String course   Palladian window
Double doors   Two full storeys
Bay window

LANDSCAPING: Anything natural and indigenous; also exotics.

DEPENDENCIES: Attached ell; freestanding.

WINDOWS: Many types of decoratives. Main windows are flat headed
    with large lights, generally one light above, one below. Single-
    or double-hung sash. Round headed; triangular; semi-circular;
    Palladian.

DOOR: Single- or double-leafed door with glass light. Fancy panels,
    some may be round headed.

ROOF: Main building block might have flat, hip, hip and ridge, or
    gabled. Tower may be helm, pyramidal, etc.

COLOR: Bi-color, with soft earth colors, soft yellow, cream, gray,
    tan. Contrasting trim but not white. Strong earth colors not
    used with this mode.

TRIM: Many classical features allowed with this style. See char-
    acteristics above.

CHIMNEY: Brick. May be enriched with fancy courses.

FABRIC: Wood on Cape (often masonry off Cape). When shingles
    are used, there may be ten or twelve inches to weather.

FOUNDATION: Brick. High, may have cellar storey.

The two Italian styles that we glimpsed on stage in the last
chapter were never earth-shakers, but they enjoyed a solid

popularity during the middle years of the 1800s. Among Historic and National Register listings we find a goodly number of examples of the two styles. Almost all Cape towns still have several Italian Villas, but the Tuscan Villa type is now scarce.

It is impossible to know how many have been lost to modernizations, but from old photographs and from poking around on back roads, we guess that there were once many dozens of these charming imports, and they were far more popular modes than present evidence would lead us to believe.

These two Italianate feature players help us see the patterning of stylistic change, and the ebb and flux of horizontal and vertical forms, of symmetrical and asymmetrical emphasis that has been the tidal movement of our architectural history.

The Italian Villa was a high flyer of the Picturesque era of building, which was part of the Romantic movement. The basic structure was composed of a group of clearly stated boxy rectangles that were severe enough to hold up under an amazing amount of decorative trim.

There was always a tower that emphasized asymmetry and added a touch of mystery and drama. Most windows were sash windows of three or four lights, that is, two lights above and two below or two above and one below. There were also decorative windows, and a large house might display occulis, triangular, round headed, semi-circular and Palladian windows among others. These, being relatively small, could be filled with "common" glass.

From earliest Colonial days, even at Jamestown in 1608, the settlers had tried to make glass. The raw materials were here but the skill was on the far side of the ocean. After the Revolution we made some progress out of stark necessity, and we were able to make small pieces of common glass for windows.

By 1825, Deming Jarves had established, in Sandwich, the Boston and Sandwich Glass Company, where he made glass household items of beauty and color that have never been surpassed. Plate glass remained beyond American abilities. By 1850 we could make common glass in sizes as large as 24 × 24 inches, and as soon as such impressive lights were available, people wanted them in order to get ahead of their neighbors, the Joneses.

But unless you could afford imported glass, you looked at the birds and the flowers in your yard through crinkles and bubbles and color flaws. When your friends walked down the street they appeared to you to shrink and grow, bulge and stretch, not unlike the mirror images that you see in the Fun House at the Fair. (Such glass now commands a premium price.) Not until 1895 could we make plate glass for windows in commercially successful quantities.

The main body of the Italian Villa often had a flat roof, and for trim — besides the multiplicity of window shapes — there were classical columns, pediments, Gothic labels, Federal porticos and quoins, consol brackets, eave brackets, modillions, look-out rafters, and verandas in every possible place. This is one of the eclectic styles that people sometimes lump together under the sunshade of "Victorian."

A style is not a cookie cutter that drops from the sky. In painting, music, acting, public speaking, rug hooking or any creative process, a style develops and is given a designation when a manner of working has components that are recognized as belonging together, and through repetition become accepted as a unit.

You do not need to recognize each mode on sight in the way that you need to name all of your first cousins at a family picnic, but it is important to know that there are many styles. Each fulfilled a need and a purpose in its time, and although they share certain minor details, each has its identity, its definitive differences, and each has meaning. But if you do get to differentiate them, you can dazzle your friends with your erudition.

Our old friend, Seth, had a brother, Russell, who was a blacksmith. When Russell and Mabel were planning their future together, Mabel saw a picture of an Italian Villa in *Harper's* magazine. She talked about it so warmly and so often that Russell had to promise to build her one in order to bring her attention back to his needs.

Mabel at once wrote of the projected Italian Villa to her

sister, Myra, who lived in Ohio. Myra's husband, George, was a successful coal dealer. By return mail Myra wrote that she and George had already laid the brick foundation for their Italian Villa. George's position in town, Myra felt, deserved The Best. This news made Mabel's hair curl and Russell's head ache.

Mabel wrote that blacksmithing was every bit as important as coal dealing, and certainly healthier. Myra replied tauntingly, asking where would a blacksmith be without coal and an obliging dealer to deliver it, and the battle was engaged.

Myra's house had a tower with an occulis window. Mabel countered with a Palladian window in her tower. Myra ran for a dictionary to look up "Palladian." Realizing that it was too late for her to build a second tower, she did manage two verandas, one on the south corner and one on the west.

Mabel wrote that she had four fireplaces, and Myra came back that anyone who did not have a good coal furnace needed four fireplaces and that she was sending Mabel some warm drawers for Christmas.

Their letters announcing that each had an indoor privy crossed in the mail. There was no plumbing, you understand, but at least you didn't need to light the oil lantern and put on boots when there was a snowy night.

Myra joined the Woman's Club and George soon after that got eight new customers. So Mabel got an oval glass for the front door and she also begged for and got an organ for the Parlor. George couldn't see what an organ had to do with the situation, but when he noticed how much energy Myra used playing Methodist hymns, he decided the organ had been a good investment.

Out of sight in this contention was the origin of this intriguing style. It was based on the simple and asymmetrical Italian farmhouse and it was "discovered" by English architects who reworked it and gussied it up for their fancy clients. They also did a really remarkable job of giving it a solid richness and consistency. Some folk thought Greek Revival too plain, others found the Gothic too informal. The Italian Villa had a wealthy-dowager air and it could carry an immense amount of architectural jewelry without seeming overdressed.

The mode arrived in Philadelphia from England and it received an enthusiastic welcome from American architects. They introduced the style to all the best people. Architects were now being accepted as paid professionals here, and they were having a field day. Books and periodicals quickly disseminated the basics and the details of the style.

This Tuscan Villa clearly shows its relationship both to the palazzi of northern Italy and also to the Georgian style which was derived from the palazzi.

It is strongly horizontal, with belt courses, a full length veranda, wide welcoming steps and a flat roof. It is also emphatically symmetrical. No outbuildings show to lessen the impact of the careful planning of the building.

The windows are long and narrow, with large lights, and the middle window upstairs has a segmental heading. The over-windows add to the horizontality and to the symmetry. The door is double leafed with engraved glass inserts.

For trim there are colossal pilasters at the corners of the building. Note that the trim continues around the house and is not confined to the front. There are many paired brackets and a belt course under the eaves. There are columns on the veranda and pilasters beside the door, with a segmental arch above.

In time past there were decorative iron railings on the roof, above the veranda and around the yard. The roof is flat and has two fire clay chimney pots. The fabric is fine clapboard, but the two shades of gray that were appropriate to the style have faded.

The foundation is of middle height; the lattice work below the veranda is a pleasant touch. This style has great dignity and propriety.

Historical characteristics of the Tuscan Villa on Cape Cod

DEFINITIVE CHARACTERISTICS:

Symmetry	Flat-headed windows
Boxy rectangle	Post and lintel doorway
Deep eaves	Veranda or balcony
Low or flat roof	Bi-coloration
Horizontal emphasis	

YEARS ON CAPE COD: 1855 – 1875 and on

GENERAL CHARACTERISTICS:

High foundation	Grouped windows
Ornate chimney pots	Window surrounds
Mutules	String course
Brackets	Double doors
Columns	Door hoods
Pilasters	Large windows
Frieze decoration	

LANDSCAPING: Stiffly symmetrical plantings. Fencing became more ornate at this time; included spacing for visibility and ventilation; built of random rubble, iron, or wood, painted to match house.

DEPENDENCIES: Ell to rear or freestanding. Will not compete with main building in placement or size.

WINDOWS: Flat headed; tall and narrow; three or four lights. Central window on upper floor may be decorative.

DOORS: Generally double-leafed doors with fancy glass inserts that are round headed.

ROOF: Flat or nearly flat, with deep overhang; (flat is defined as a rise of not more than one in a run of twenty).

COLOR: Softer light colors most appropriate here; gray, tan, stone color, soft yellow, dark red, with contrasting or bi-color trim.

TRIM: Belt courses (same as string course), brackets, balcony, full-length veranda, window hoods, door hoods, balustrades, roof combs, fancy chimney pots, quoins, mutules, dentils, pilasters, columns, fancy fencing repeated on balcony and roof. Verandas were popular then and added shelter, storage, shadows, summer cooling and sitting space. They often ran the full length of the house and around to the side. Verandas also added horizontal stress, which appeals to Cape Codders and fits in with the landscape.

CHIMNEY: Ornate fire clay; ornate brick; multiple; symmetrically placed.

FABRIC: Wood, shingle or clapboard.

FOUNDATION: High; brick. May contain kitchen level, with windows near ground.

In less than ten years the Tuscan Villa had also come via the same route — Florence, London, and Philadelphia — but this was a very different Pappa Al Pomodoro. A child of the town rather than of the countryside, the Tuscan Villa is a tight, anti-picturesque, symmetrical entity based on the Tuscan Palazzi that gave us our Georgian style. The two Italians may share a flat roof, many roof brackets and an immense dignity, but there the resemblance ends.

In the Tuscan Villa horizontality is emphasized with stiff front-yard fencing, full-length balconies, belt courses and roof combs. Fancy windows are rare. There will be two storeys on Cape, three in domestic examples off Cape, and five or six in commercial buildings. But no more than that; for remember, we didn't begin to have have elevators for people before 1861. But we did have freight elevators.

The doorway was central and on each storey the windows were directly above those of the lower level. Again, it is hard to know how many Tuscan Villas there once were on the Cape, because Tuscan is, in its basics, a dressed up Georgian, and one who is easily persuaded to disrobe.

But the Tuscan interior can tell you something with higher ceilings than older styles and with richer trim. For floor plans the asymmetric styles — that is, the original Gothic and the two Gothic revivals — used the side entrance plan, and so did the Italian Villa. The Georgian used the central doorway and so did the Tuscan Villa, with a long passageway opposite the door.

You enter through the double-leaf doors that were so popular at the time. These might be of Sandwich glass, engraved with handsomely etched designs of flowers and birds, swirls and ribbons.

There will be a room-door to the right and one to your left. Overdoors may be quite ornate and have entablatures and pediments.

To one side of the entrance is the slow rising staircase of dark varnished woodwork, with an enriched newel, heavy handrail and turned balusters.

The high ceilings may have heavy plaster rosettes for lamps (oil, of course), and we may find a tin ceiling or two. Tin is a soft metal and is easily pressed into low relief pattern. In the second half of the 1800s this was quite a popular and inexpensive way to add decoration to a room. Slick-paper catalogues offered, besides ceilings, whole walls, panels, and dadoes in Classic, Roccoco or Gothic modes, with as many as four hundred patterns to chose from.

The upstairs did not have closets, which came late to Cape Cod, replacing the traditional wardrobe largely after 1900. But upstairs was a staircase to the flat roof, from which there was often a stupendous view. In those years the Cape was largely deforested and on a clear day you could see from High Brewster to East Orleans, from Harwich to Dennis, and across the Cape in many places.

The roof had a handsomely turned railing and balusters and one or generally two fire clay chimney pots. These pots were ordered from another catalogue which offered hundreds of choices, from simply pargeted stacks to voluptuously curved pots of amazing contours. These were of cream, tan or rust color and added a nice termination to the appearance of the roof. Under the eaves could be heard the monotonous murmurings of pigeons, to whom the many eave brackets were Happy Honeymoon Cottages.

Downstairs, at the back of the passageway, we would find the dining room. In a corner was the dumb waiter, for this was the era of the cellar kitchen. Not that autumnal-harvest kitchen of the Upper Cape Georgian, but a dark, probably dank and surely depressing work area for servants sometimes, but more often where mama herself could grind away the hours with the perimeter of the room always in shadow and the cupboards smelling musty.

Oh, take us back to the cheerful above-ground kitchen, with children screeching in and out, with papa coming in from the barn to hook a fresh doughnut, with Aunt Carrie stopping by to gossip and staying to help with the raspberry jam, and the sweet song of the catbird on the windowsill.

CHAPTER TWELVE

The many-sided Mr. Fowler and the Octagon style

This Octagon, although modest in its statement, has the requisite stucco walls; the windows are symmetrically placed in the facets of the exterior; the roof is flat and crowned by a fire clay chimney (in place of the more usual cupola) and at each corner is a gutter system and downspout that contribute to the health of the roof.

The front door has an excellent hood with handsome ancones and turned drops; above is an iron railing that gives a balcony effect. At the side is a veranda leading to the back door.

The outbuilding is consistent with an octagonal shape and here we find the cupola which gives good ventilation and a pleasant termination to the structure.

These buildings are of considerable historic value and deserve appreciation and admiration as a demonstration of the Cape Codders' awareness of the off-Cape world. After more than a century, the lines stand true and are a tribute to Orson Squire Fowler's construction principles.

Historical characteristics of the Octagon style on Cape Cod

DEFINITIVE CHARACTERISTIC: Octagonal shape.

YEARS ON CAPE COD: 1865 – 1880 and on

GENERAL CHARACTERISTICS:

Low or flat roof pitch	Balcony
Belvedere	Door hood
Masonry construction	Brackets
Wrap-around veranda	

LANDSCAPING: Any indigenous plantings, also exotics.

DEPENDENCIES: Seldom attached; outbuildings may also be octagonal.

WINDOWS: Flat headed; a few decoratives.

DOORS: Compatible with style of building.

ROOF: Low or flat.

COLOR: Soft light colors only. Rich earth colors not used on Cape. Tan, gray, cream or mottled to resemble stucco.

TRIM: Generally not too conspicuous. Any style of the era was used, but Gothic the most favored.

CHIMNEY: Generally there was a central chimney rising from the center of the roof or against the cupola.

FABRIC: Cement, concrete, stucco, brick or something made to simulate one of these.

FOUNDATION: Masonry, rather high due to a cellar storey.

N umbers are part of the fabric of our daily lives. We play the lottery, count the strokes when beating a cake, watch our speedometer and memorize our social security number. Some numbers seem to have more significance than others. The number three is of particular interest around the world, and we find that triads in art and religion are common.

To medieval man numbers had important symbolism and were a limited language, well understood by those who could not read script. To medieval man four was the terrestrial number and was related to the four cardinal points of the compass and the four natural elements (air, water, fire and earth). Three was the spiritual number, the number of the Holy Trinity in Christian belief, and so the figure of Christ-divine was often shown as upheld by the four Evangelists, symbols of earthly matters.

Medieval man further believed that to multiply the divine number of three by the earthly number of four was to infuse the mundane with the spiritual and the number thus achieved, twelve, signified the Holy Church and its twelve Apostles.

To add three and four produced the fascinating result of seven, which has always been a controversial digit and is the one that expresses the dual nature of man that wars within him, the seven sins that plague him, the seven virtues that comfort him, and the seven planets that influence his destiny.

The number eight denoted rebirth, for it is the number of man plus the added one of spiritual life. For this reason baptisteries and baptismal fonts are often eight-sided, thus signifying the opportunity open to man through baptism.

Numerology takes a different view and considers the number eight to be the businessman's number, bringing worldly success through worldly attitudes. Music sides with the medievals, for the western musical scale is divided into octaves and each eighth note is a new beginning.

Buildings that have eight sides, whether for religious, artistic or any symbolic reason, have occurred rarely but steadily throughout our history. Around 100 B.C. the Athenians built an octagonal temple to the eight principal winds. It contained a sun dial and a water clock.

The lovely chapel of St. Vitale at Ravenna is eight-sided. Charlemagne in 805 A.D. made an eight-sided chapel at Aachen. There are many octagonal baptisteries at Cremona, Rome, and Florence (where the baptistery has the super bronze doors by Ghiberti). In America, at Washington, D.C., Dr. William Thornton designed an octagonal residence for Colonel John Taloe; George Washington had several eight-sided summer houses at Mt. Vernon; and Thomas Jefferson and Frank Lloyd Wright are among the architects who used this intriguing form. Around 1850 the octagonal shape caught the fancy of that remarkable man, Orson Squire Fowler.

The western world in the early 1800s saw a rising concern by people for people. Fuller stomachs and increased financial and political security allowed large numbers of just ordinary folk to give an increased consideration to the well-being of themselves and of others. The First International Workingman's Conference was held. The United States engaged in a Civil War partly because of concern by some for the condition of their less fortunate brothers.

Many men whose names have since become household words — Adam Smith, John Stuart Mill, John Dewey, Andre Marie Ampere, Georg Ohm, Rudolph Diesel, Louis Pasteur, Goodyear,

Bessemer, Bell — and an almost endless list of great minds cast their thoughts into the pool of men's needs. The results affected the physical, mental, industrial, psychological and intellectual aspects of the lives of millions who had never heard of these disturbing thinkers.

Architecture is immediately responsive to what is happening. The architecture of the mid 1800s began to give constructive thought to the situation of the poor man, of the rural family and of the woman who could not afford domestic help.

Publications of the day offered plans for simple cottages and considered matters of price, ventilation, sanitation and convenience, and then gave do-it-yourself instructions. Orson Squire Fowler was a prime mover of this new viewpoint.

The idea of planning a house, whatever its size, for the comfort and convenience of the occupants was not usual. We have watched the earliest settlers, who sought a sense of stability through having everyone build as his neighbor did, achieving a stronger feeling of community through anonymity of facade. This gave us the Cape Cod Cottage, which was in those early days really the New England Cottage and maybe even the East Coast Cottage, because its simple medieval facade was built from Maine into the Carolinas.

But the Cottage could grow to fit the immediate needs of its dwellers and its flexibility was spasmodic not mandated, and achieved some eventual individuality. The Georgian, for all of its exterior planning, was far less amenable to the requirements of its occupants.

Now, as the population became more mobile, the pendulum swungs again. In the second half of the 1800s, Americans found the maturity to go home and visit their ancestors. European travel, European study and European books gave us information that brought a dozen modes home.

City jobs attracted many folk. Certainly many Cape Codders went to the cities to find work and excitement, more companionship and, they hoped, a freer way of life. But city life was not like home, and as these people got older, married and raised families, they yearned for a bit of green to come home to, a place to grow a few ears of corn and have a couple of chickens.

This urge created the suburbs. Trolley car lines and railroad stations were built to meet the need for transportation.

Orson Squire Fowler was a vivid expression of his time. He was strongly conscious of the problems and needs of his generation and he devised many far-sighted solutions. He was an eccentric, a professional phrenologist, reading character from the bumps on your head, which was all the rage in those days. He was married three times, wrote sex manuals and gave marital advice.

Fowler's enthusiasms were magnanimous and his convictions powered his enterprises with a two-hundred-and-twenty-volt current. He decided that the octagon shape was the panacea for all the problems that afflict architectural design and by extension most of the troubles of the world.

A gravel wall, which he considered the perfect building material, was a combination of gravel, sand and lime, and was "everywhere abundant." To extend his gospel to all who might need it, he wrote a book called *The Octagon, A Home For All*, which quickly went to eight printings. The book vibrates with Fowler's intensity about domestic issues and he spreads the umbrella of his concern over a wide range of related topics.

Fowler tells us how to construct his gravel wall, giving many but not complete instructions. He claims that many materials can be used, suggesting brickbats, blacksmith's siftings, coal dross and ship's ballast as vehicles for the sand and lime.

His enthusiasm then goes bounding off to batter boards, window framing, chimneys, scaffoldings and roofs, always leaving some of the details to the reader. Although he is said to have done much of the work on his own sixty-room, four-storey octagon at Fishkill, New York, you feel that much was left by Fowler of necessity to professionals. He gives a recipe for making gravel wall look like granite by painting it with pigment, iron filings and salt.

Fowler firmly believed that everyone should have a house to live in and that the home should promote the health, happiness and welfare of the family and contribute to the well-being of the community and thus the prosperity of the nation. He would feel vindicated in his views if he could see how far our present lack of caring for the home and family unit has taken us in the opposite direction.

His book gives instructions for the laborer, who may earn only twelve dollars a month, to save four dollars per month toward the purchase of a home by going on the Fowler Diet, which he claims to be entirely adequate and healthy. Fowler was a vegetarian, but you wonder if he ever tried anything as extreme as his own advice. "Buy," he says, "a bushel of wheat and two bushels of apples. This will supply a man and his wife with a month's food." He says to boil the wheat and add the apples, sometimes cooked, sometimes raw for variety. This menu speaks of a man for whom the end often eclipses the means.

He further says that a man, no matter how poor, who has worked all of his life to earn a reputation for honesty, will find some person, perhaps a farmer with a good deal of land, to sell for five or ten dollars, a plot that would be refused to a "less honorable petitioner."

Fowler suggests that really poor people build multiple dwellings. Although some of what he says fits a simpler day, much of his book can be of serious value to someone building a home today.

In discussing the many facets of healthy, happy living, Fowler recommends the planting of fruit trees and berry bushes. He advocates that each child have his own bedroom, because this fosters responsibility, independence and good study habits. He suggests a play room for children where they may romp and yell in a natural manner. He also suggests a gymnastic room for females who, in those less relaxed times, could not bounce down the boulevard in a bikini.

He believed that exercise might save many a person from a premature grave and also restore invalids to health. "Mankind," he says in his enthusiastic way, "are dying off like diseased sheep from pure ennui. They want ACTION."

He advocates that the outhouse be brought indoors for the sake of invalids and the elderly, and his arguments are clear and effective. He speaks of the need to recycle waste materials and suggests preparing for the time when the earth will have a larger population than it can feed.

Fowler carries the octagon banner to schools in which the teacher can easily oversee all of the pupils and in which the nearly circular shape will establish a magnetic and electrical rapport that will enhance learning.

Churches built in Fowler's favorite shape will be pleasanter places, he claims, for rather than looking at the back of the heads of the other members of the congregation, folks will see something of the faces around them and thus benefit from a sense of companionship. He includes many floor plans in his book.

Among the virtues that he cites for octagonal houses is that the ratio of floor to wall is greater than in a conventional plan, thus being less expensive. Here he is undoubtedly correct. The octagon gives easy access to all rooms, with no space wasted in passageways, and he sponsors a central staircase lighted by a cupola in the roof.

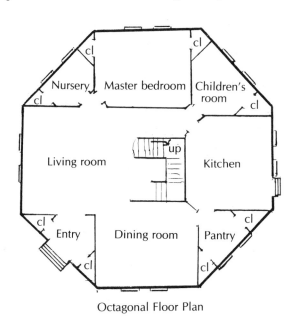

Octagonal Floor Plan

For these reasons the house is easily heated, ventilation is good and the housewife is saved many steps. All acute angles, he says, can be made into closets.

Back when people had fewer extraneous goods, no beach umbrellas, no movie projectors, evening wraps, or tennis rackets to store, closets were few and the wardrobe held your Sunday suit. So closets were one of Fowler's many constructive ideas. Even when the pitcher of his enthusiasm ran over and even slopped on the table a bit, most of what he wrote was creative and was already or would soon be needed.

Hundreds and then thousands of octagon buildings rose across the land and Cape Cod had her full share, although only a handful remain. And if you look around you will find that in the past five years Cape Cod has acquired a number of new octagon homes, all of which are very handsome.

Those who did not build in this form frequently did incorporate Fowler's excellent ideas into the more standard types. But the shape proved hard to resell. Under Fowler's compelling logic, YOU wanted an octagon and you loved it after you built it, but when the boss sent you to another city to live, and you put your octagon on the market, buyers hesitated, untouched by the enthusiasm that had charmed you. So the basic idea fell off for a hundred years, but the splendid suggestions relative to it have lived on and been incorporated into homes ever since.

Stylistically there was no norm. Fowler himself seems to have favored the First Gothic Revival type of trim, but home owners built according to any and all of the modes then crowding on the scene, the style in each case being modified by the contours of the octagon.

On Cape the octagon was of two stories (three or more being common off Cape), with a central stairwell and a low-pitched or flat roof topped off by a cupola. This sometimes gives the impression that the house is a giant's cookie jar. Windows were symmetrically placed in each face of the building. This shape lends itself easily to balconies and wrap-around verandas and these soften the angularity and emphasize the traditional Cape Cod horizontality.

Fowler's book was an immediate success, either because of, or in spite of, his ornate and dramatic language. His basic premises expressed concern for humanity, considering human welfare and showing a genuine caring for facts and details of living that were then usually ignored.

His influence is not to be questioned and goes far beyond the octagon that he so loved. His fervor was contagious and his respect and affection for the home, for individual privacy, for personal needs, for comfort and health were an important leavening in the life of the 1800s in all of America as well as on Cape Cod.

France gets dressed for her fall — The Second Empire style

This is the ultimate in Second Empire, a distilled essence of the mode. The outbuildings are in style and so reinforce the main building. The landscaping is minimal and the fencing is a bit of extended house-decoration. Although this mode is generally vertical and often asymmetrical, our example does not lose by being strongly horizontal and absolutely symmetrical.

The lower windows have rigidly horizontal hoods and the upstairs windows are enclosed in delectable little porticoes with wedding cake pediments. There is a bay window on the side. The entrance portico, with gold-topped Corinthian capitals, clearly shows the Roman background of this style. (The Greeks did not care for Corinthian, thinking it too ornate.) The perfect rhythm of the modillions is a delight, and the trim sets up a musical cadence that is well controlled by the quoins.

The roof is the quintessential mansard with a lantern on the top, and the upper slope of the roof reminds you of its presence with small pedimented windows.

The soft yellow color is entirely consistent with the fashion, the classical trim is white, and the roof is striped in two close shades of red.

The fabric — including the quoin blocks, which here are purely decorative — is wood. In a masonry building quoins are supportive and stabilizing. The foundation is low. This building is a thorough joy and an example of superb workmanship.

Historical characteristics of the Second Empire style on Cape Cod

DEFINITIVE CHARACTERISTICS:
  Mansard roof
  Eave brackets
  Fancy window surrounds

YEARS ON CAPE COD: 1865 – 1880

GENERAL CHARACTERISTICS:

Bay window	Ancones
High foundation	Classical trim
Portico	Mutules
Columns	Dentils
Modillions	Tall sculptural chimney
Quoins	Belvedere
Articulated silhouette	Tall windows with large
Bi-coloration	lights
Door hoods	
One and a half, two, or two	
and a half storeys	

LANDSCAPING: Natural or formal; often minimal. Trees are a great asset to this style.

DEPENDENCIES: Ell to rear, out of sight; also freestanding. Outbuildings will also have mansard roof.

WINDOWS: On Cape these are generally flat-topped on lower floor, round-headed on upper floor. Upper floor windows are generally smaller than those on lower floor and have decorative surrounds. Lower windows generally have four lights.

DOORS: Main door is important feature. It will have door hood with ancones or portico with columns. Balusters are infrequent. Door may be double door (very popular then), with glass lights in upper halves.

ROOF: The mansard roof is definitive for this style. In restrained types it indicates intention if not fulfillment. Upper pitch may not be visible from ground; lower pitch may be bell-curved or almost vertical. Lower pitch is sometimes treated as part of the wall and this is indicated by coloring lower pitch to match wall rather than to match upper pitch. Decorative parti-colored shingles used to make patterns.

COLOR: This style requires soft earth colors, with earth color trim. Pastels never acceptable and white sparsely used in trim. Roof may be red or green or parti-colored. Gray or natural.

TRIM: Decorative trim of classical derivation, with columns, pilasters, consol brackets, finials, and enriched window surrounds.

CHIMNEY: Of brick or fire clay; tall and sculptural, adding to feeling of richness and height.

FABRIC: On Cape almost unfailingly of clapboard; if shingle, probably a later change.

FOUNDATION: Brick; high, may have cellar kitchen.

One of the many modes that Cape Cod has adopted with great success is the Second Empire style, the one that we recognize by the mansard roof.

When you look up through the dark foliage of century-old elms and see the gentle slopes of the mansard, you are looking at a chapter in our architectural history. You are also looking across the Atlantic to the story of a despotic emperor and his beautiful empress.

French ties to Cape Cod started when the fishermen of the French seacoast began, at least by the year 1500, to sail east across the Atlantic to fish on these shores. The vast quantities of cod and haddock made the long sail worthwhile by putting sous in the pocket and supper on the table. One fisherman in the 1500s wrote of having made sixty Atlantic crossings during his working years.

In 1606 the French explorer, Samuel de Champlain, spent several weeks on Cape Cod. He made maps and left descriptions of harbors and bays and of Indian customs.

Later, after the Cape was settled, there were migrations from here to Nova Scotia and thereafter there was much trading, visiting and intermarriage between Cape Codders and French Canadians. Boudreaus, Belliveaus, and D'Entremonts are part of the Cape, just as Nova Scotia telephone books list Nickersons, Eldredges (and Eldridges), Dyers, Riches, Bournes and Sparrows. I am not purposely ignoring the Goulds and the Doanes or anyone else, but you can't list all the Cape Cod families without writing another telephone book.

During the Revolution, during the War of 1812 and ever since, Cape Codders have traded with France. And as France warmly welcomed Benjamin Franklin, Elijah Cobb and Charles Lindbergh, we have happily received the Marquis de Lafayette, Alexis de Tocqueville and Gerard d'Abouville.

In 1852, President Louis Napoleon Bonaparte of France became Emperor Louis Napoleon the Third, and the Second Empire was established. For some years Fortune seemed to be emptying her cornucopia of blessings for the benefit of the new monarch and his country. France's financial tactics were progressive. Railroads, shipping companies, and utilities developed; there was an active social policy and conditions for working men improved. France's technological abilities grew and she became the mightiest of nations. Paris was a world center of culture, splendid architecture and elegant living. The essence of this reputation still clings to France and her capital.

Louis Napoleon appointed Baron Georges Eugene Haussmann to dress Paris in the latest fashions. Haussmann did this and went even further — he set a few fashions himself. He was a city planner par excellence and he widened the streets into great boulevards, planted thousands of trees, relocated railroad stations, improved traffic circulation, and created vistas and open spaces to give a dramatic approach to monuments. Many magnificent buildings were built to add to the beauty of the city.

For some time past, much of the western world had been building in Greek Revival style as an expression of democracy and freedom, as a departure from the immediate past and as an associative link with the distant past. All of the Napoleons saw themselves as Roman Caesars, thus it was to the imperial qualities of the late Roman architecture rather than to the more restrained and moderate nature of Athenian democracy that France turned for creative inspiration.

The style that was favored was one that already existed but

had been done only sparingly. Under Haussmann this mode, with its mansard roof, was given a baroque enrichment, and the courtly and hierarchical nature of Louis' reign, with its dramatic ceremonies and stately assemblies, was reflected in the architecture.

It certainly was impressive.

England and France had just won the Crimean War (1856) against Russia, and France was regarded as the greatest of military powers, the mightiest of nations. Paris was *the* world center of culture, and so it followed that this grandiloquent architectural style was copied throughout the western world.

In 1852 Louis had married Eugenie de Montijo, Countess of Teba and daughter of a Spanish grandee. Those who saw Eugenie said that she was exceptionally beautiful, those who knew her considered her simple and gracious, those who had to deal with her found her ideologies to be unreasonably conservative. Such reinforcement to the native self-importance of her husband did not help the cause of reforms that France still needed so badly.

Had Louis kept his early promises to his people that they would have increased self-determination and had he used his power within his own country, history would have portrayed him as a beneficent and constructive ruler. But his despotic inclinations and political greed led him to war with Italy and then with Germany. Suddenly Fortune's cornucopia was indeed empty and at the bottom was disaster for Louis, for Eugenie and for France.

When the emperor and empress had been swept away (in 1871) and when France was at last freed from German occupation, the beauty and splendid restructuring of Paris largely remained.

In those days America met every boat that brought a new style, hugged the style as it came off the gangplank, introduced it to the press and to society and then scanned the periodicals for the next arrival. During the 1860s, political and social changes in America were asking for new architectural modes.

The Greek Revival that so many had taken so warmly to their hearts now seemed rather ingenuous and was not acceptable to the powers that were arising in the cities. Here were industrial and political emperors with invisible crowns whose empires were growing like Jack's beanstalk.

These men welcomed the showy and dramatic facades of the Second Empire to demonstrate their own sense of importance and to impress their public. Suburbs were growing, and narrow lots allowed this style, which went to three or four or even five storeys (plenty of stairs will keep your maids from getting stiff in the knees), to add a long ell into the back yard for extra interior space.

Impressive and ornate, many of these houses still stand and now are sometimes painted purple or pink. They are handsome when well kept, when neglected they have the air of a tired dowager who has a bit of petticoat hanging and an untidy coiffure.

On Cape this style was welcomed with a sort of well-we-make-our-chowder-to-suit-ourselves attitude. Cape Codders threw out the tomatoes and added salt pork and onions. They took the often gangling mode, lowered the roof line, lightened the sometimes somber coloring, set the building among trees rather than in a dry, angular cityscape, and mitigated the often too-ornate trim. This accomplished a beauty and dignity that, although greatly pared down, harked back somehow to the French original. The result was another terrific tribute to the innate Cape Cod sense of appropriateness.

While all Cape towns have some Second Empire buildings, and their appearance runs from interesting to gorgeous, Provincetown is the Queen of the style. The mode was popular on Cape after 1870 and in the years between 1870 and 1890 Provincetown's population grew by a thousand people and about two hundred new homes were built. Fishing had fallen off throughout most of the Cape, but in Provincetown, with her famous fishing fleet of glorious schooners with their clipper bows and tapered sterns, fishing remained a profitable trade. It followed of course that some of the building done at this time should be in the popular and not inexpensive Second Empire style.

The mansard roof is handsome against the sky and the only possible criticism of this mode as you now find it is the ubiquitous white paint. The present century is determined to paint every possible surface white and accent it with dark shutters and a dark roof. This preoccupation is hard to understand.

The variety, the softness of gray and cream, of muted red, gentle yellows and browns that made our towns so good to look at, has been replaced by monotonous and glaring white.

No one thought about color in the 1600s; color was whatever resulted from using natural materials. In the 1700s, on Cape Cod, stone gray, Indian red and brown were within reach, at the very least for the Town Meeting House. In the 1800s, except for Greek Revival, which was generally believed to mandate white, all the rich earth colors were used and generally with contrasting, not white, trim. (Pastels came here in the late 1920s.)

This was because the styles called for these colors — white being considered in those years "unnatural" — but also because people in small towns and rural areas yearn for color. Color fulfills a need for enrichment of the scene and adds an individual touch. Thoreau speaks happily of the red roofs of Cape Cod and of the cheer that they engendered. Hurrah for Thoreau, hurrah for color, and hurrah for the Second Empire and her gift to Cape Cod.

CHAPTER FOURTEEN

A well deserved tribute —
Queen Anne style and the
Bracketed style

And here is good Queen Anne. The building is horizontal and it is asymmetrical. The outbuildings are in
keeping with the mode and attractive in their own right.
They are to the rear so as not to intrude upon the handsome lines of the main building.

The windows, while of general consistency, are of many shapes and sizes, each designed to fit a special wall surface. The door is shadowed and has a large oval light.

The roof consists of many angles and although it is "busy," it is held in place by the quiet color. It climbs to a climax in the delightful turret. There is variety in the dormers and they work well together.

The color is green with cream trim and the choice is excellent. The trim itself is minimal and consists of the wrap-around lines, the gentle contours, the lookout rafters, the squatty columns and the reeding of the veranda railing. The columns do not rest uneasily on the veranda railing, but are supported on shingled bases. I am forced into using superlatives when I describe this house. It is the finest restoration I have seen on the Cape. For quality of workmanship and consideration for the original building, I don't see how you could surpass it. This house is a credit to the owner and to the town in which it is located.

Historical characteristics of the Queen Anne style on Cape Cod

DEFINITIVE CHARACTERISTICS:

Irregularity of plan	Corner veranda
Queen Anne windows	Many roof angles
Turret	

TIME ON CAPE COD: 1885 – 1920 and on

GENERAL CHARACTERISTICS:

Diapered shingles	Stickwork
Bi-coloration	Casement windows

Jetties	Squatty columns
Deep eaves	Balcony
Pedimented gables	Tabernacle
High foundation	Variegated textures
Articulated silhouette	Tall, sculptural chimneys

LANDSCAPING: Asymmetrical, informal. Fencing now became more formal and private; made of random rubble, evergreens, brick, wood, stone; often up to eight feet in height, according to size of lot. At the drive entrance there were often tall posts, with lower fencing that was sometimes reinforced by greenery.

DEPENDENCIES: Generally freestanding.

WINDOWS: Large-paned, single- or double-hung; Queen Anne windows; decoratives.

DOORS: Not of great significance. Queen Anne type in upper half of door; wood; fancy metal doorknobs.

ROOF: Articulated; many roof angles; many pitches from low to steep; dormers; conical roof on tower; Sussex hip (also called Hipped Back or Jerkin Head) often used.

COLOR: This period is still in the bi-color years and in the era of the richer earth hues, with more variety than previous styles. Dark green with cream; yellow with orange; two shades of green. Green has now made the scene but blue is too new; for Cape exteriors, blue is a twentieth century hue. Roof colors coordinate with walls, often being darker but similar.

TRIM: Queen Anne can be very simple or most ornate. A wrap-around veranda is almost mandatory; also a turret or close-hauled tower. All trim is of one color, generally cream (not white), and the shingles are natural; or there can be a large amount of classically derived ornament, but columns are short and fat.

CHIMNEY: Queen Anne gets the prize for tall, fancy chimneys, with cutouts, ornamental courses, cartouches, and sculptured brickwork.

FABRIC: On Cape almost unfailingly of wood, clapboard being favored and shingle taking second place.

FOUNDATION: Brick; often high, indicating a cellar storey.

I n the early days of settling New England and Cape Cod, the law said that no one could live alone. It was understood that one of the basic needs of humankind is to belong, and the most natural thing to which we belong is the family. If you had no family of your own, you were required to join one, and legally you were counted as a member of that household.

As part of that family you shared in the plenty and the scarcity, the sadness and the triumph. When the well went dry, you helped to dig a new well, and if you were ill, someone brought you chicken soup and an extra blanket.

The idea of the family as a security net, as a powerhouse and as a road map was a vital part of our history until after the time period covered by this writing. It was the compass that gave people direction and the courage to sail ahead. The limiting tendrils of the familial vine, although seen as a restraint in youth, in hindsight were regarded as the taproot of happy living.

Home was a magic place. When you came to the back door and slipped off your boots, you saw in the window the small white card with the pointer that told the ice man how much ice was wanted tomorrow. In the pantry was the brown wooden icebox itself, with chrome handles and with hinges turning green.

The old dog knew your step and his tail was already thumping his bit of rug behind the stove. When you came into the kitchen he rose rheumatically and followed you. Above the black soapstone sink, the brass faucets gleamed, and in front of the sink the linoleum was worn thin by the feet of family members who had stood there washing dishes from thousands of meals.

In the dining room with the cabbage rose wall paper, the

oval table was set for cold Sunday night supper; the baby's highchair was to the left of mother's seat and on the table, under the chandelier, was the salt cellar, the pepper shaker, the spoon holder and the sugar bowl from the Philadelphia World's Fair. At each place was a cloth napkin in its individual napkin ring.

The upright piano was open in the living room and a hymn book lay on the rack. Through the wide windows came the joyous sounds of the family and neighbors playing sandlot baseball.

On the porch, grandma sat in her favorite wooden rocker and the old dog slipped down next to her with a contented sigh. At grandma's feet were half a dozen baskets of beach plums that she was picking through.

"Have some cider," grams said, flicking a finger at the green pitcher. You took a glass, poured some cider and eased into the rocker next to hers. You were home.

The domestic architecture of the 1800s expressed the idea of home with a sittable veranda, many bedrooms and glistening windows of different shapes and sizes. No style did this better than Queen Anne. The style started in England in the 1860s, came to America (landing in Philadelphia, of course) in the mid 1870s and became popular on Cape in the 1890s and thereafter.

In those years the Cape was becoming a busy place. The railroad had reached all the towns, taking Cape cabbages to market and bringing in tourists with a different brand of greenery in their pockets.

Hotels and stores grew to accommodate the summer visitors. Restaurants and ice cream shops opened and employed young people, while husbands and fathers went finfishing and shellfishing, and grew turnips in Eastham, strawberries in Falmouth and cranberries almost everywhere. During the winter the Life Saving Service gave employment to the finest and bravest of men who risked their lives and often saved the lives of others for sixty dollars a month and "found" (i.e., housing and meals).

Many people were building homes in these years. The Greek Revival had crested and the picturesque styles were now in vogue.

Not everyone needed to build, but they did want to be in style. Many took their Cape Cod House or Cape Cod Cottage and "Queen Anned" it with great success. A close, low tower was easily added, along with some windows containing colored inserts, a veranda or two and perhaps a balcony to give an enriching shadow. Soft paint colors were applied and the trick was done. We were right up there with the Joneses.

Queen Anne herself was, from all accounts, a good woman and several constructive things happened during her reign, but the style that is named after her is not quite typical of what was being built in her day. However, the name is pleasant and above all is a fair tribute to a most domestic woman who did her best to fulfill her duties by having sixteen children. Sadly, she outlived them all, most of them having died in infancy.

Good Queen Anne, you are indeed a fine example of home and hearth.

The Bracketed style is a house for three generations and its homey appearance is welcoming. The landscaping is a good background. The windows are the two over two of the period and there is the traditional round-headed window in the gable end.

The door is double leaved to accommodate the ladies clothing of the time. "Now crinoline is all the rage, A petticoat made like a cage, Tis formed of hoops and bars of steel, and worn by girls to be genteel" goes an old song of the 1870s. Our example has a wooden screen door, and above the door is a door hood. This hood is supported on the wonderful ancones which exactly match the paired brackets that are tucked wherever possible around the facade.

This style is asymmetrical and mildly horizontal. The window hoods cast a slight but welcome shadow, and there is the characteristic bay window.

The corner veranda has vines that provide summer shade and privacy and there is a full complement of brackets. The foundation is low, the fabric is clapboard, and the trim and detail are not limited to the facade but run around the building in a happy prosperity.

The chimneys are minimal. On the interior the rooms are high-ceilinged, with dark woodwork and enriching wallpaper. The whole building speaks of domesticity, hospitality and our mislaid sense of family.

Historical characteristics of the Bracketed style on Cape Cod

DEFINITIVE CHARACTERISTICS:

Brackets	Veranda
Asymmetry	Bay window

TIME ON CAPE COD: 1860 – 1900

GENERAL CHARACTERISTICS:

Narrow window hoods	Gazebo
Modillions	Door hood with ancones
Round-headed window	Numerous eave brackets
Flat-topped windows	

LANDSCAPING: This style was often part of a farm-home complex and had typical farmyard plantings, including fruit trees, and a good deal of picket fencing.

DEPENDENCIES: Extensions might go to as many as six or eight farm buildings, often attached, with the barn being last in line; also freestanding.

WINDOWS: Flat-topped, single- or double-hung, with small or large panes. Very often two panes above and two below. Round-headed window in gable end; occulis.

DOORS: May be single wooden door, with square glass insert above; double-leaf doors with fancy glass inserts. Door hood with ancones; portico with pediment but seldom with balusters.

ROOF: Gabled; may have based pediment. Often there are several gables because this style resembles several closely held rectangles.

COLOR: Soft earth colors with contrasting trim, especially gray, soft yellow, tan, cream.

TRIM: Brackets or modillions under eaves; brackets under and over windows, around veranda, under pediment. Brackets generally simple in shape and sometimes in groups of two or more, as well as single.

CHIMNEY: Brick; simple; tall and skinny.

FABRIC: Wood, almost always clapboard.

FOUNDATION: Brick; high.

A fashion that greatly ornaments the Cape is the Bracketed Style. Some architectural historians don't mention it. Some assign to it Italian parentage. It is highly eclectic and has some resemblance to the Gothic, the Italianates and to Queen Anne.

That in its simplicity it still has a clear-cut identity, is an interesting comment on all of our overlapping modes. We can see how a lay person, confused, can lump all of these together as "Victorian," but Victorian is far more a viewpoint than a fashion, and for the discerning House-Peeper, using this terminology is a cop out.

Most of the styles done on Cape are minimal in their presentation, but this does not keep them from expressing individuality. In some ways it clarifies, for in order to qualify for a specific designation the mode needs basic characteristics which therefore reduce it to a standard.

You cannot miss Bracketed on Cape Cod or elsewhere. And when you see it, you may agree that its homey, cozy, attractive appearance puts it close to Queen Anne and makes it one of our more domestic modes.

Perhaps we should call it American and have done with it. We can find it not only on Cape but throughout New England and across the West. It once was even the mainstay of the New Jersey suburbs. Its foreign parentage seems doubtful.

The house is a basic rectangle and extensions are close to the main body of the house. There is an off-center door which may be, on Cape, a double-leafed door with sandblasted inserts. Over the door is a door hood with turned brackets called ancones. These are a delight. Their variety displays almost infinite imagination and beauty, and you will go many a mile before finding two alike.

The veranda is to the front or to the side of the building and practically demands the accompaniment of a trumpet vine or wisteria. There is a bay window. The roof line is quiet, the chimney inconspicuous. In the gable end will be a fancy window that is almost always round-headed.

Of course the building has brackets under the eaves, under the windows, under window hoods, around the veranda and under the bay. But don't be fooled if there are no brackets at all. Time often eliminates them because they hold moisture and rot and then are not always replaced. Without brackets the style can still hold its own, and house-peeping, like bird watching, is habituating.

Bracketed has a wonderful air of friendliness and middle-class domesticity. Unfortunately, today it is often painted white, which does it an injustice. White paint not only is out of keeping with the era, but also makes the building seem too bulky and fails to show off the trim. As an alternative, two soft shades of gray, can emphasize the clean lines and the delicate detail, and this lessens the appearance of mass.

As you come in the front door of Queen Anne or Bracketed, you will find the stairs on one wall of the entrance passageway. The other wall has the door to the sitting room, where you will find the bay window. The passageway ends at the kitchen, which is roomy and has several pantries. ("Pantry" comes from the French word *pain* ("bread"), and the word "buttery" comes from the French word meaning "to bottle," hence "bottler" and then "butler.")

Bracketed uses the same excited wallpaper as does the Queen Anne and the same dark varnished woodwork with deep mop boards. Ceiling heights run around eight feet and this can make a small room seem boxy. Many Cape Codders grew up in the security of these sturdy walls.

CHAPTER FIFTEEN

Another jovial Henry — Richardson Romanesque

This Richardson Romanesque library is most satisfactory. It is asymmetrical in plan but horizontal in stress. This proclaims its admirable adaptation to Cape Cod, for in urban areas this mode is quite often vertical, and that would not fit our landscape.

The tall trees are a benefit here as they are to all large buildings. There are slit windows, eyebrow windows and some of the windows have stone transoms.

The wide arched entrance is made dramatic by its shading, which also marks its importance. There is a sunny bastion which gives articulation and adds interest both inside and out.

The entire building is subtly polychromatic, with several warm close colors of masonry. The keystone and the voussoirs of the great Roman arch are different from the brickwork and the belt courses above. In one gable end there is a coffer with diamond-patterned brickwork. The slight color changes break up the mass of the building and soften its impact in a subliminal way.

The foundation is high, of gray granite and battered. It is in random ashlar. The feeling of strength and purpose provided by this style is well suited to the building's use.

Historical characteristics of Richardson Romanesque on Cape Cod

DEFINITIVE CHARACTERISTICS:

Bi-color	Roman arch
Massive, weighty	Asymmetry

YEARS ON CAPE COD: 1880 – 1890 and on

GENERAL CHARACTERISTICS:

Masonry	Flat-topped windows
Battered walls	Cruciform windows
Slit windows	Arched entry
Eyebrow windows	Round-headed windows
Tower	Bastion

LANDSCAPING: No specifics; often minimal.

DEPENDENCIES: Ell or freestanding.

WINDOWS: Flat topped, round headed, occulis, slit, eyebrow.

DOOR: Arched entry; massive, wood.

ROOF: Gabled, of various pitches; generally of slate. Suitable roofs for towers, etc.

COLOR: Two shades or colors of masonry; third color might be for trim. Wood trim of cream or gray, tan or brown.

TRIM: Roman arches; decorative windows; shadows.

CHIMNEY: Masonry, not conspicuous.

FABRIC: Masonry; brick; wood.

FOUNDATION: High, with cellar storey; probably battered.

One of the most interesting aspects of any creation is that which the work tells us about the creator. Who would doubt that Van Gogh was full of eerie passions, who would question that Wagner was a man of strong convictions or that Debussy was shy and sensitive. Read just one play of George Bernard Shaw and you see that he was sophisticated, individualistic and had a sense of humor like a hat pin.

When we look at the architecture of Henry Hobson Richardson, we see evidence of a man who was strong, dependable, determined and with many other old-fashioned virtues.

Although he built civic centers, libraries, railroad stations and other buildings to last, unfortunately he himself did not. He died at the age of forty-eight, but the work that he had already done was sufficient in power and direction to place him among America's most influential architects. Sullivan and Wright, both of whom he preceded, acknowledged their debt to him.

Richardson was the second American to sign in for architectural studies at the Beaux Arts in Paris, and he worked there until the Civil War cut his funds from home and he could no longer earn enough to continue his training. He came home, set up in his profession in Boston, and then won the competition for the design of Trinity Church there. After that his career was on assured ground.

When we speak of an architectural revival some prejudice seems to attach, as though the architect involved could not walk without a crutch. No man can make something from nothing, and no architect can learn his trade without studying the work of past builders. Then, in spite of himself, he likes some forms better than others, and he puts into his own creations some of the spirit, detail and even basics of that which he admires.

Richardson found something to which he felt akin in the calm security of the French Romanesque. There was a compatibility of strength, dependability and determination that was like the man himself. Identifying with this type of construction, he interpreted it well, put it into keeping with contemporary needs, and made it his own personal expression with great success.

Richardson Romanesque was popular and it was done by many other architects, although by none so notably as Richardson himself. For public buildings the style had particular appeal, although some larger homes have been done in the mode. Richardson Romanesque gives a sense of permanence, structural soundness, masculine beauty and rightness for its purpose. Richardson did courthouses and jails with excellent results.

The round-headed Roman arch is at the bottom of the whole thing. And at the top and the middle, too. The Greeks didn't have it. Their work was post and lintel, massive, straight-edged rectangles of stone and marble, yielding rectangular buildings. To achieve height or to make a covered way, the Greeks used the corbel.

Rome learned from her older neighbor, Greece, and without Grecian workmanship from which to spring, Rome's artistic summer would not have been so fruitful. But Rome found a winning number in the architectural lottery and won the jackpot with — of all things — a brick. Small, handheld, easily transported, cheap to make, the versatile brick had the right combination of characteristics as a building material.

With the brick, Rome had at its command arches, high ceilings, bridges, domes, tunnels, and curves. Wherever Rome went, which was both wide and far, the brick could be toted along or brick material readily found at hand on location.

Bricks made roads, too, that carried Roman armies, generals, merchants and artisans all over the western world. The Roman arch was a triumph and it remained supreme in building until our old friend, Archbishop Suger, raised the roof with the Gothic arch.

The Roman arch is limited in how high it can go, but the Gothic arch can go up almost indefinitely and it has a grace that the other lacks. But the rounded arch has hung in there and it is still a vital part of construction everywhere.

Greece "fell," as they say in the history books, and Rome carried on. Too much carrying on caused Rome to fall in its turn, and even when Rome had ceased to be an important power, the magnificent constructions remained as tangible evidence of the past.

Many of the great Roman buildings were vandalized to make new buildings by people who were smart enough to admire but not clever enough to originate. But many other structures stood through the long centuries of political and artistic winter. The massive and sturdy creations of Rome dominated the landscape and offered a waiting source of inspiration to whomever should come along to be inspired.

As European life restructured itself during medieval years, much building was based upon the ruins that Rome had bequeathed. When the French Normans invaded England, the castles, keeps, monasteries and churches that were subsequently built in England in Romanesque terms were called Norman. (The Normans conquered England fifteen years before Suger was born.)

It was all based on the Roman arch and done with large blocks of stone. The concept of the brick had been mislaid, perhaps because it was small. Now the brick began to stir itself up out of the mud and demand to be counted.

Because it took the Normans quite a while to subdue all of

England and the political atmosphere was aggressive, fenestration was minimal and the resulting buildings were sturdy, massive, lasting, defensive and decidedly gloomy.

In France, where the political picture was less tense, the Romanesque was romantic and dramatic as well as sturdy. Here Richardson saw it and was impressed with all of the previously mentioned virtues. He brought these architectural gems home in his head — thus avoiding any problems at customs — and worked his own magic with them. Greece gave to Rome, Rome gave to Romanesque and Romanesque gave to Richardson.

Richardson Romanesque was not widely done on the Cape. There has been little call for structures of such substance, but we are fortunate to have some examples and these are fine, although not of his personal creation.

They are a tribute to Cape Codders who, far from being insular on their peninsula, were always interested in the world around them, aware of the flow and movement of life, sensitive to changing times and well capable of expressing on home ground not only the great Cape Cod Cottage and Cape Cod House, but all the wonderful and progressive pageant of architectural history that pertained to their time.

CHAPTER SIXTEEN

Sticks without stones —
The English style

The Cape has a number of complexes in this reminiscent mode. They are corner properties with shops on the lower level and living accommodations above. There are also many single shops throughout the Cape that use this nostalgic exterior to achieve attention.

Domestic examples abound and run from English types that ramble over the landscape with many roof angles and clustered chimneys, through stucco homes that remind us of the 1930s. There is at least one house whose stickwork has a strong oriental flavor.

This example has trees that soften the height, although how trees can live without soil from which to obtain food and water, I do not know. The windows are plain, the doors recessed, the gables are steep and establish a rhythm that is kept from monotony by having different patterning in each gable.

The color is proper to the style, with cream walls and dark brown stickwork which constitutes the trim of the building. The chimneys are clustered as they would be in the original Tudor Half Timbering style.

This is a satisfactory way to do a shop on the Cape and a number of most successful new homes have been built in this mode in recent years.

Historical characteristics of Stick style or English style or Tudor Half Timbering on Cape Cod

DEFINITIVE CHARACTERISTICS: Decorative stickwork.
YEARS ON CAPE COD: 1890 ongoing
GENERAL CHARACTERISTICS:

Bi-coloration	Weightiness
Fancy chimneys	Rectangularity
Bays	Horizontality
Jetties	Queen Anne windows
Diagonal bracings	Flat-headed windows
Pedimented gables	Casement windows

Pillars   Lower masonry storey

Many roof angles   Deep eaves

Variety of texture

LANDSCAPING: This was an era of replanting trees in a bare landscape.

DEPENDENCIES: Attached at rear or freestanding.

WINDOWS: Flat headed, small paned; casement; Queen Anne; occulis.

DOOR: Not a significant feature. Wood; simple panels.

ROOF: Many roof angles; low pitch; steep gables; wood or slate; articulated.

COLOR: Tan or gray or cream; dark brown stickwork.

TRIM: Stickwork; diagonal bracings. Rich shadows result from articulation of facade and roof and patterning of the sticks.

CHIMNEY: Multiple; Elizabethan clusters; decorative courses but not conspicuous placement.

FABRIC: Clapboard; brick; stucco.

FOUNDATION: Not high.

Stick style may not seem like an exciting name, and yet this fashion has had one of the most exciting histories. In the seven hundred years since the basic style first developed, it has twice risen from retirement like some great actress who, rejuvenated and recharged with vitality, has played again a leading role.

When Stick style was done on Cape Cod it was called English style and surely this is an appropriate name, for its origin is English. But the name of Stick is something with which we are stuck and truly a rose, even if called a turnip, would smell as sweet. (We are not putting down the Cape Cod turnip, a delectable vegetable of which the Cape is justly proud.)

Observing houses is not unlike observing birds. It is well to know that the bird singing in your lilac bush is a sparrow, but it is more satisfactory to know by its markings and its notes that it is a song sparrow. To recognize the wild flowers when you go for a walk, to know something of the composer when you listen to a symphony, all of these add to the flavor of life.

This is also true of houses. To know that your Cape Cod home was built in the 1800s is great; to comprehend the story of its characteristics, to learn the why and when of your home, gives an added dimension and a deepened quality to ownership.

So how do we recognize and understand Stick style?

We have noted man's struggle to make a roof that would not collapse and then to sustain this roof upon walls, thus creating a weatherproof, full head room domicile. To do this it was necessary to invent the ground sill, wall framing, the collar tie, king post, roof tree and wind bracing. When these components were together assembled, the basic goal was achieved and people set about building houses in quantity equal to the demand.

Wood, large wood, was then plentiful in England. The framing was made of massive timbers, and plenty of them. Wall studding was often placed twelve inches on center, that is, from the center of one stud to the center of the next was twelve inches. Floor boards and roof boards were often three inches thick or more.

Between the studs the wall was composed of cob or plaster of local composition, and each housewright had his own secret formula. Ingredients would include clay, animal droppings, road scrapings, grasses and so on. This cob was supported on a woven mat of twigs and small branches that lay between the studs. The depth of the stud was the depth of the wall.

The cob filling turned white or gray or cream, according to its contents, and this showed on the outside of the building between the dark woodwork of the framing. The effect was vivid, and in time people patterned their houseframing with diagonals, herring bone patterns, and other repetitives. The startling contrast of creamy walls sustained on dark wood is one of the most eye-catching enrichments of English and European architecture.

To this was added the drama of projecting oriels and also

the jetty or overhang. Both of these items enhanced the picture, for they cast wonderful shadows and gave gentle articulation to the silhouette with a sort of "opulent restraint."

When Henry the seventh, he of Star Chamber infamy, was on the throne, this mode was a rising child actor. His son, the corpulent Henry the eighth, found this fashion to be an ingenue of talent. His daughter, Good Queen Bess, who tried to conceal the onslaught of time with many pearls and mighty ruffs, saw this style in its maturity and thought it an excellent stage setting for her political machinations. These three members of the House of Tudor gave their family name to this form of building: Tudor Half Timbering. This was the original of which our Stick style is a revival.

Supply is putty in the hands of demand. In 1349 at Mecombe Regis in England, a vessel discharged a passenger whose name was death. Death set out, traveling through the towns and the cities, gathering up all ages and conditions of folk without any discrimination. The only criterion was that the victim's flesh must be tasty to the flea, the same flea that also liked rats.

Half the population qualified — and died. In those days everybody had fleas; even kings and queens had 'em.

This plague gave a low blow to feudalism, for landowners could not find enough workers and the workers who were left had bargaining power. As the situation adjusted itself and England turned to sheep farming, which enormously improved her economy, we find the formation of that sturdy spine of civilization, the wonderful and indispensible middle class.

These people wanted homes, nice homes. And they could pay for them. This caused the profession of housewright to prosper and it also — since houses were now often built by professionals rather than the householder himself — raised the standards of construction. Many fine homes of half timbering were built in these and following years, and England today is a handsomer place as a result. These houses were built to last.

The jetty deserves a word. Myths have grown up around the

jetty, as they grow around any subject when men of imagination are not sure of the answer to a question. Myths are valuable contrivances. If your small son asks you what makes the thunder, you may hesitate at the technical answer. But if you tell him about the great god, Thor, beating out the tremendous shields and swords and helmets for his fellow gods, the kid's eyes will glow, and who can guarantee which explanation is the myth.

So jetties have been explained as giving more space on the second floor, as protecting the man in the street from the emptying of slop jars — "Gardez-loo," the chamber maid used to call as she let the contents of the chamber pot fly out the window. In America the jetty supposedly allowed you to pour boiling oil on Indians and other enemies.

We assume that the Indian waited patiently right under the slot (if there was one) in the jetty floor, while you struggled up the ladder with a pan of boiling oil and then poured it down on him before it cooled. Such a stunt was more likely to burn you than the enemy.

The evidence in hand tells us this is what happened: English housewrights in the 1400s or so did not take high school physics, nor did they go to trade school. So for several hundred years — which is not long as things go in learning how to build houses — joists were laid on the flat instead of on edge.

Even with joists three inches thick, laying them on the flat causes bouncy floors. Extending the joists out for a foot and raising the second floor on this extension does much to stabilize the joists. The joists were laid the width of the house and the jetty the length, and the teazle post and the dragon beam helped to hold up the jetty. On late examples of the style, and after joists were laid on edge, the jetty was continued for its own attractive sake.

The New England settlers were familiar, of course, with half timbering as they had seen it in their native land and in Holland too, for the fashion had penetrated all of Europe. It was tried in New England, particularly in western Massachusetts and Connecticut, and some was done in Boston and its environs. In eastern

Massachusetts it was not at all successful. First you have to season your lumber a long time, and few folks could wait for that. Recipes for cob did not work well here, and the wood and the cob soon parted company. People found that a tight skin of shingles was the best thing for local houses. In a few pockets in Connecticut this fashion was continued into the 1700s, but it just didn't suit our climate. Such half-timbered houses as were built were soon covered with shingles, as we find when such houses are demolished. We also find that these houses often had their joists laid on the flat.

Associating the term "garrison" with the jetty is also a misconception. The true garrison house is built of massive beams, mortised together, rather than pinned boards, and this construction is not evident from the outside. Houses built with massive framework are a good place to be when hostilities are rampant, but records clearly show that most garrison houses used for protection in the years of the Indian Wars were of one storey. If they were of two storeys and did have a jetty, this was happenstance. Garrison houses were built in upper New York state and in western Massachusetts, scene of the French and Indian Wars. A jetty on Cape Cod clearly proclaims itself of 1900s vintage, for they were not built here until then.

After the Civil War, when Americans began to rediscover Europe, they swarmed eastward, whence their ancestors had earlier struggled westward. On shipboard, in place of the wooden bucket, they had tile baths; instead of sour water, moldy cheese and wormy biscuit, they had iced drinks and delicate finger food served by starched stewards.

In Europe, Americans gazed upon baroque palaces, romantic ruins, and transcendental cathedrals, and they marveled. Suddenly history mattered. American interest in the arts exceeded home production and Europe became a grab bag. Although the new enthusiasm for the arts was notable, discrimination was at times less than commendable.

Soon a Persian Palace arose beside the Hudson River, and a

semi-Moorish confection stood among pine trees. Bizarre concoc-
tions of styles, periods and geographical settings found structural
togetherness under a single roof and the product would often be
architectural babble.

But our new Paris-trained architects used their drafting tables
to lessen the commotion and they led us among the accepted
styles.

And there, waiting in the wings, poised, sure of her welcome,
was our Tudor Half Timbering, about to be renamed (by the
architectural historian, Vincent Scully) the Stick style. She was the
stellar answer to Europhiles and Anglophiles.

This mode is highly associative. It is picturesque. In our mind's
eye we see Mr. Pepys leaning out of his window to watch the
great fire of London. We see the mighty Dr. Johnson, seated at a
tavern table under a small, diamond-paned casement window,
dispensing aphoristic gems by the light of a candle. Oliver Gold-
smith nods agreement, and James Boswell slips quietly out of the
massive, iron-bound door to seek a young girl for dalliance.

The Philadelphia Centennial Exposition of 1876 did much to
popularize the style in this country and of course Cape Cod is
never left behind for long in anything. Wood, quiet color, natural
textures and simplicity are all appropriate to our landscape and to
our thinking. Summer residents in particular built Stick style along
the shore, in large lots back from the road, and the results were
most pleasant.

It is characteristic of any stylistic revival that what is structural
in the original is merely decorative overlay in the revival, and
nowhere is this more evident than in Stick style. The great "sticks,"
the massive timbers that sustained the house in Tudor days, were
both the structure and the decoration, and without them the house
would be "just another house." In the revival the "sticks" were
just superficial patterning, and yet they remain indispensible, for
without them the house would be "just another house."

The style held its popularity for many years, and much of

what was done on Cape ran into the 1900s. It has a quiet richness, it is a sober style and it is always proper.

Stick style is still being done on Cape as well as in other places, and the style has held up well over the years. No other fashion has changed so little in its appearance. It still has presence and still blends in well with our landscape. Whatever you may chose to call it, Stick is still one of the Cape's more indigenous modes.

CHAPTER SEVENTEEN

An American classic —
The Shingle style

This is a classic example of the Shingle Style. The wide gable end is an important characteristic and so are the jettied windows that add so much articulation to the gables. The shingle-clad veranda pillars, with their arched terminations, and the shingled arrises are definitive of the mode and give stability to the sweep of the roof.

Shrubs shield the house from the road. Outbuildings are unobtrusive and do not distract from the handsome house. The windows are plain, and we see three at varying levels that tell us where the stairway is. The doorway is sheltered.

The deep eaves of the roof and the slow slope of the dormer give horizontal emphasis, and all the lines of the house are restful. The trim is confined to the lookout rafters and to the deep shadows that provide the subtle coloration.

This house was once symmetrical. The window on the far left has replaced a veranda that was identical to the present veranda on the right, making two entrances. Originally the interior was that of a mirror house, with a party wall dividing the house vertically into two duplexes and with one floor plan being a flip-over of the other.

Historical characteristics of the Shingle style on Cape Cod

DEFINITIVE CHARACTERISTICS:
   Broad gable ends
   Shingle-capped arrises
   Horizontality
TIME ON CAPE COD: 1880 – 1920 and on
GENERAL CHARACTERISTICS:

Deep shadows	Eyebrow windows
Jettied windows	Tabernacle

Casement windows   Modest chimney

Diapered shingles   Curves

Balcony   Belt course

Many roof angles   Arched veranda pillars

Many window shapes   One and a half to two

Many window levels   storeys

Porte cochere   Semi-circular windows

LANDSCAPING: Varied. Fencing was now on holiday and was often replaced by privet hedging which might be quite high.

DEPENDENCIES: Both ells and freestanding, the latter more usual.

WINDOWS: Queen Anne; casement; flat topped; ribbon; oriel; generally large lights. Windows were often on different levels, sometimes suggesting the rise of stairs, with three windows in a close row going up the side of the house. Windows often had a semi-eliptical shingle hood at top and were jettied out at bottom.

DOOR: Not a major feature. Wood, simple, with glass insert at top.

ROOF: Most conspicuous and definitive feature is that the gable end is the wide side of the house, the front of the house being comparatively narrow. Fanciful towers and turrets; bell shapes; gambrel; varied pitches.

COLOR: Natural shingle only. Trim may be cream by preference, or gray or brown.

TRIM: This mode has no decoration other than fancy windows and fanciful roof shapes, shadows and arched veranda pillars. Belt course may continue around building, following curves, and should not be white.

CHIMNEY: Large and plain; seldom busy.

FABRIC: Wood shingle.

FOUNDATION: Often high; masonry. Masonry may continue up to include arched veranda pillars.

S hingle Style is a fashion that fits beautifully into our Cape Cod landscape. It is an asset not only to many private homes but to public structures.

The public buildings of Cape Cod are no less handsome and no less important to our story than the justly admired domestic architecture. Cape Codders, like all New Englanders, have always taken their religion and their learning with intense seriousness. Their Meeting Houses, libraries and churches have benefited accordingly.

The Meeting Houses of the 1600s and the 1700s have not survived except, in a few instances, where vestigial bits have been incorporated into newer structures. Building on the Upper Cape in the 1600s and on the Lower Cape in the 1700s was seldom of lasting quality, heresy though you may consider this to be. In reading old accounts we find that although the best workmanship available was put into the Meeting Houses, after twenty or thirty years the Meeting Houses were beyond repair and had to be replaced from scratch. By the 1800s, when people started to build churches, the time, money, material and talent were on hand.

The statement that a Meeting House is not a church may need a word of clarification. In the early days on Cape Cod — and by early days we mean here almost the first two hundred years — you *were* a Congregationalist. If you wanted to vote, to do business and to have the warm handshake of your neighbor, you went to Congregational Meeting every Sunday. Every householder paid taxes to support the Congregational Minister, his parsonage and the Meeting House, which was the scene on Sunday of religious services and during the week of secular activities. Here civic matters were discussed, argued, voted, rediscussed and reargued. And maybe even revoted.

The Quakers were the first to intrude into this self-dedicated fraternity. The Quakers were on their way from Boston, where they were sometimes hanged, to Plymouth, whence they were chased, to Cape Cod, where they were more kindly greeted before quickly passing on to Rhode Island, where they were accepted before they moved along to Philadelphia, where they blossomed.

In England, in the 1700s, the chasuble of the Church of England had raveled somewhat at the hem. People became seriously disputatious even to the point of dying for what would seem to us today to be doctrinal trivialities.

One group set themselves aside and said that they were Methodists. These people disagreed among themselves and broke into New Connections, Primitive Methodists, Bible Christians, Wesleyan Methodists and Wesleyan Reformers. Some folk became concerned with ways of baptising; these Baptists split into nineteen subdivisions. Members of these strong-minded denominations crossed the Atlantic and eventually landed on Cape Cod. Clearly they were not Congregationalists. So why, they asked pugnaciously and not without reason, should they support the Congregationalist Minister, his growing family, his Parsonage and the Meeting House?

When the heat of battle had subsided and after some folk had gone so far as to tear down each other's place of worship — and yes, I do mean on Cape Cod — church and state had separated. Each denomination then built its own church and each town built its own Town Meeting House to be used for secular matters only. True, each householder now had two places to support, but rancor was lessened and religious freedom had made a big step forward.

All of this was happening after the turn into the 1800s, when the Greek Revival and First Gothic Revival were popular. Thus it is not surprising that many of our lovely churches were constructed in one of these two styles or at least had doors and windows and trim that pertained to these styles. The third most popular style for Cape Cod churches, the Shingle Style, came a bit later.

Shingle Style is generally conceded to be an American concoction that was fathered by the American architect, William Ralph Emerson, silverspooned by Henry Hobson Richardson (who worked in styles other than Romanesque), godfathered by McKim, Mead and White, "uncled" by Henry Paston Clark, Bruce Price, Lamb and Rich, and once even dandled on the knee of Frank Lloyd

Wright, who did some Shingle Style at Oak Park in 1889.

The late 1800s, as we have seen, was a time of flamboyant architecture. In the cities this was for some people a time of burgeoning wealth, opulent spending and ostentatious social one-up-man-ship. Shingle Style is a simple form, restrained in color and detail. When a few million-dollar "cottages" were built in this mode at Newport, part of its appeal seemed to lie in a sort of reverse snobbery on the part of people who felt so rich that they could afford to mitigate display.

Interiors were designed with long sections of wall omitted to give a flowing informality of space, in which living rooms blended into sitting rooms, dining rooms and on out to sun parlors. This freedom of internal movement was pleasing to contemporary social attitudes and gave a good background for lavish hospitality.

The openness provided additional light, which helped to offset the gloom of deep-colored wallpapers, dark varnished woodwork and heavy velvet portieres and drapes.

This fluid interior needed a free-flowing skin on the outside, which did much to dictate the wrap-around lines of the Shingle Style. We find in books and magazines of the day, floor plans for Eastern Seaboard houses with a range of social rooms that are placed to enjoy the water view. The dining rooms show seating arrangements for many guests, fifty or more in the ornate examples. Upstairs are bedrooms, sometimes twelve or more — and one bathroom. After a long, large meal that probably included much wine, those guests must have had a few problems.

Now it became fashionable for inlanders, even those of modest means, to go to the seashore for the summer or at least for the choice month of August.

On Cape Cod some of these folks built Shingle Style summer homes that had plenty of room for all the family and for their numerous friends. The spacious interiors were cool and pleasant, the housekeeping simple and the upkeep inexpensive, since nothing had to be painted but a bit of plain trim.

Inns developed and literally grew as businesses expanded to

meet the vacationing demands of those who did not chose to build for themselves. The long, relaxed body of Shingle Style was perfect for rural inns. There were ample verandas for the Rocking Chair Brigade, and large, airy dining rooms for those slowly eaten, many-coursed, home-cooked meals. The menus were handwritten and the waitress did not give you her name because you already knew it. You had few choices for the main course: either fried oysters, boiled lobster or quahog pie. You could have all three desserts if you wished, and the bill at the end of the week for room and board was six dollars per person.

The high ceilinged bedrooms were cool and the dark wood-work required little dusting and hid all but the most egregious of spiders. The maids worked fourteen hours a day and hurried down the corridors with an unending procession of chamber pots concealed under white cloths whose edges flapped in the breeze.

Cape Codders liked Shingle Style. It looked like home to them. The lines were low, the colors soft and the textures natural. It was reminiscent of their Cape Cod Cottage and Cape Cod House, from which, in fact, it took much of its heritage. It was roomy enough for a couple of summer boarders, too.

Summer visitors were proper people and they went to church, and all over the Cape the collection plates reflected their attendance. More churches were built, often in summer-use areas, and these were frequently in the prevailing mode of Shingle Style. Sometimes Gothic lines were borrowed, resulting in Gothic arched windows and shingle-clad buttresses, and on the interior we find dark stickwork against a light background.

The generous sharing between styles during the 1800s produced remarkably little hodge-podge and resulted in so many clearly defined modes, but all this can be confusing at first. To recognize each fashion easily is fun, but it is not of paramount importance. To see the forces behind each change is of more consequence.

Each style rose to fulfill a need, to express a contemporary viewpoint, to demonstrate the history of social thrust, financial fluctuations, new techniques, and new materials, and to record these patterns in tangible form. Architecture is a history book with which you cannot tamper.

There is more to Shingle Style itself than a gracious interior enclosed by compatible shingles. One feature that is seldom shared with other modes is that the length of the building is often the gabled side, and not the lower eaved front.

Windows may be on slightly differing levels and they may be individually jettied out. Veranda pillars may be shingle-clad and are almost always arched at the top. All possible arrises are shingle covered with Boston corners.

To paint this style is to blaspheme it. The soft gray of the shingles, with the seductive dark accents of dormer, balcony, jettied windows and tabernacles, gives it its great beauty. When you add a cream-colored satiny ribbon of fascia board that follows, caresses and delineates the undulations, you have Shingle Style at its most opulent. This is truly American architecture that earns our fullest admiration and respect.

CHAPTER EIGHTEEN

A home from home —
the Bungalow

This bungalow has much of the atmosphere of the Indian Bangla from which it sprang — more, perhaps, than the type of bungalow with which we are generally familiar. The breadth of the roof and the simplicity of the veranda pillars are partly responsible for this. The low foundation and the wide steps also help.

The plantings add wonderfully to the horizontality and the ell does not detract. The garage, although fronting the road, is planned to be unobtrusive, unlike many modern garages that become the blatant theme of a property and dominate the scene.

Both the windows and the door are simple. The dormers are less obvious in fact than in the picture, and could be brought into greater relationship with the roof through protective coloration.

There is the essential chimney. The total is gracious, relaxed and in thorough keeping with the landscape both in line and in tone. A bungalow has tremendous charm and sometimes the statement is so low-key that we must pause and study it to recognize its value.

Historical characteristics of the Bungalow on Cape Cod

DEFINITIVE CHARACTERISTICS:

Low, one or one and a half storeys	Veranda
	Chimney
Natural texture	
Natural color	

YEARS ON CAPE COD: 1890 – 1930 and on

GENERAL CHARACTERISTICS:

Balcony	Casement windows
Tabernacle	Box or collection of boxes
Dormers	Natural landscaping
Flat-topped windows	Close plantings

LANDSCAPING: Generally plenty of close plantings. Random rubble fencing.

DEPENDENCIES: Often freestanding garage. May have acquired ells later.

WINDOWS: Flat topped and casement prevail; flat topped will have large lights, often one over one.

DOORS: Not a main feature. Wood, generally with glass insert.

ROOF: Gabled; hip; hip and ridge; low pitch; sometimes collection of roofs of same pitch; dormers; jerkin head.

COLOR: Natural; dark brown, dark green. Light colors were seldom used.

TRIM: Structural trim. Veranda pillars of random rubble or brick. Shutters may have decorative feature.

CHIMNEY: Considered necessary for the style, since this was often a second home and the fireplace provided all of the heat. Wide and plain, not high.

FABRIC: Wood; stone; stucco; brick; logs.

FOUNDATION: Low; masonry; sometimes covered over with wood.

The Bungalow, which came to us from India, was enormously popular because it filled a need, as we shall see. It usefulness stemmed in part from the breakup of the three-generation family.

When our friend, Seth, back in 1855, built that Greek Revival house for his lovely Mehitabel, he was driving a delivery wagon for his father's market. Seth was a real nice fellow and he did many errands on the side for the customers. In those days it was not easy to get into town. You could walk, or get a ride with a neighbor, or you could take the horse — if you had one and it was not plowing or haying time.

So Seth would bring you some thread or some cough medicine from Doc Gifford, and his father's business — what with Seth's good nature and the policy of "first-class merchandise sold cheap" and not much competition anyway — did well. True, they did "lose the post office" when the administration changed, but when Seth was elected Selectman, things got better than ever.

Seth's grandson enlarged the store, put on a new facade, and made a corner for newspapers and magazines. But when Seth's great-grandson, Alfred, was graduated from high school, he refused to be the fifth generation to run the market. He said that he already knew that business from the broom up, and insisted that his professional life was going to start with a white shirt and a necktie.

His pa, Ned, admitted, with a mixture of pride and heartache, that the business could afford to send Alfred to college, but he didn't see any need for it, because look what he himself had done and with only — and so on. So Alfred went off, dressed in a three-piece suit and carrying a cowhide valise. He came back four years later with a diploma, a marked taste for beer, and a straw hat. However, he refused to wear the straw hat to go to work on the meat side of the market.

Instead he got a job at Smallhoff's Emporium for Ladies. In two years he was promoted to assistant manager and he proposed marriage to Gertrude, Mr. Smallhoff's secretary.

Now there were no flies on Gertie, as she was fond of telling folks herself, and she wasn't going to live with Al's ma and pa and all that horsehair furniture and those heavy meals. "Think of my 'figger,'" she said, and Al replied that he did, all too often.

So Al put two hundred dollars down on a Bungalow that had just been built by Cleveland Bassett from a Sears and Roebuck plan. When the young couple got back from a wedding trip to Brockton, they bought wicker furniture and Gertie made cushions and curtains of bright flowered chintz. She grilled the grapefruit for breakfast and made salad for supper. She even bobbed her hair and smoked cigarettes, things that she never could have done under the same roof with ma and her withering comments.

Alfred and Gertie got a telephone, they bought a flivver (second hand) and Al built a crystal radio set in his basement workshop. Their Bungalow was perfect for them; it was compact, attractive and expressive of their cherished independence. Within a few years pa and ma sold their big old house and bought a Bungalow right next door to Alfred, because ma could no longer climb stairs. And of course there might be grandchildren.

The story of the Bungalow starts this way. Years before, the British government had built, in India, official rest houses, stations for traveling officers, government officials and important guests. These houses, spaced about a day's march apart, were based on local architecture called Bangla.

The Bangla was a low, one storey building with wide verandas and deep eaves. On the interior the ceilings were open to the roof, showing the structure, and a wide passageway ran through the building for ventilation. The kitchen and other service rooms were separate, back in the Compound.

The Bangla was comfortable and picturesque, and caught the attention of architects, who were always looking for ideas. The first Bungalow in the United States is said to have been built in Massachusetts in 1880. For a while the definitive characteristics of the style, as it was to be done here, was up for grabs. When things settled down, the Bungalow was determined to be a low, one-storey building, the upper part to be made inhabitable only through the courtesy of dormers, with conspicuous verandas and a chimney. This last was added because the Bungalow was an especially attractive style for second homes, and the fireplace was often the only source of heat.

The popularity of this type of building was immediate and terrific. California and Florida in particular went Bungalow-mad. It filled the need for inexpensive vacation homes, it made an economical house for a small family and whole Bungalow-developments were built. Such fantastic architects as Charles and Henry Greene "did" Bungalows.

The variety was almost infinite. There were Swiss Chalet Bungalows, log cabin Bungalows, and oh!, did those have the requisite rustic quality. There were Japanese, Spanish, and Mexican Bungalows and even Pompeian ones, with great sophistication of garden rooms surrounded by fluted columns, with a fountain and a lily pool and masses of flowers. (These of course were off Cape. Here we were more conservative.)

They were built of wood, cement blocks, stucco, logs and even of canvas. Bungalows fit into all landscapes except the truly urban. They were happy in the hills, lovely at the lake and successful at the seashore.

Many publications helped the cause and made it easy to own a Bungalow. Magazines and catalogues offered floor plans and building plans for as little as five dollars. If the weather cooperated, you could build your own Bungalow-home during summer evenings and weekends. Many people did just that.

Bungalows were available for as little as five hundred dollars, which made it possible for young couples around the turn of the century and folk of limited means to own their own house. For two thousand dollars you could have a palace of a Bungalow. Plan books gave estimated prices, too.

One-storey Bungalows were inexpensive only because they were small and compact. On a cost-per-square-foot basis, the second storey of a house is far less expensive to build than the ground floor.

Published information went into detail in regard to amenities. Lighting systems were discussed, acetylene gas being one suggested source of lighting for the home. One expert said that for lighting, "sixty-eight degree gasoline [whatever that is] at eight cents per gallon can be used in a two horse power generator with a switchboard." When you needed water more than you needed light, the engine could be uncoupled from the dynamo and used for the pump. Ah yes, the good old days, when mechanics were simple and most men could handle them.

Water systems were carefully thought out and a number of options suggested. If you were able to dig a well, the hand pump over the kitchen sink could have a cutoff valve so that the drinking water need not go through the holding tank. This would appeal to me. I've seen those holding tanks in old houses.

For water disposal, a septic system with a patented gate valve and a siphon is suggested, allowing forty linear feet of three-inch tile for each person in the household.

Interiors were often fascinating. With all major rooms on the ground floor, planning was needed in order not to waste space on passageways. This was sometimes achieved by having an open plan, with the kitchen and dining room as alcoves to the main room. You also needed to be sure that the verandas did not cut off too much light to the rooms. The open plan helped reduce that problem, too.

The American Bungalow, like its original in India, often had a cathedral ceiling, and gave a great deal of impetus to this feature. The color and texture of the interior structural members added much cozy charm, especially if there was a balcony at the upper level. The hearth would be large, with a fieldstone fireplace and inglenooks, or at least high-backed settees. All this gave some of the early-American look that was so popular then and which had done much to popularize the Shingle Style.

Oriental corners were then the big thing, and Bungalows often had them. This was a bit of the room—perhaps a deep window seat, with many cushions and heavy drapes—where young folk could visit with a modicum of privacy while still being chaperoned by the older folks who were playing whist by the fire.

Even the small, box-like Bungalows, of which the Cape has many dozens, had their charm and some of this came from plantings. Publications advised you to set out vines as soon as the builders left.

There should be a winding path to the entrance, with flowers and vines. All this was when the Kudzu Vine had just landed from Japan, and a few writings suggested that you put this out for a quick cover. Some folk got more coverage than they wanted.

The verandas could be supplemented by pergolas, a porte-cochere or a grape arbor, all of which added to the horizontality and to the bucolic flavor.

In India the Bungalow walls were of masonry, due to the vast population of termites. Here wood was preferred and was often stained dark brown. The roof might be leaf green, with a tabernacled sleeping porch set in. Casement windows were frequent, and although the chimney was not featured, it was there. Today many Bungalow verandas have been enclosed to give added interior space, and also because we no longer sit on the veranda in the evening as a family and chat, sing rounds and watch the neighbors stroll by.

All of these features of the Bungalow added up to a cozy, simple, homey quality that helped to account for its widespread construction. Every town in the country had one. Every Cape Cod town had one, and most of the Cape towns had dozens. Bungalows are sometimes misunderstood and under-appreciated, but to know them is to love them.

PART THREE

Looking at your old house

CHAPTER NINETEEN

Looking at old houses —
I. The problems

It seems to be important to people to have a date for their old house. A friend told me that her neighbor, who had an old house, had begged her to bring me to tea. It was one of those late December afternoons with a swift gray sky. The melting snow and the warm east wind off the ocean combined to make the air stick to you all over. As we came up the path, the front door opened and out into the glow of the porch light stepped our hostess. She extended a warm hand of greeting.

"I am so glad that you could come," she said. "How old is my house?"

I had never been in her house before and I have not been there since, but I know that — except for Ranch houses, Garrison houses and other obvious products of the 1900s — all houses on Cape Cod are at least two hundred and fifty years old, and about one third of them are the oldest house in town. The best part is that it's hard to prove that this is not true.

Dating your old house can and should be fun. The problem lies in taking it too seriously. Dating houses is more of a problem on Cape than off for several reasons. One is that records are scarce, and when they are kept they are seldom explicit. And even when they are kept they are not always "kept." I asked for some records at a local Town Office recently and was told, "Oh, we took those to the dump; we simply ran out of space."

So if your house is, you think, more that a hundred and

twenty-five years old, be willing to settle for a good guess. After you have guessed, add on another fifty years just in case. Why not?

In earlier times communication between the Cape and the mainland lagged, and so did communication between towns on Cape. You can hear apocryphal stories such as the one about the Old Timer who knew the soundings and approaches to the Boca Tigris in Canton, but hesitated on clear directions to Harwich. Each town had a strong feeling as to its individuality. Each town had its idiosyncracies as to building.

Old Chatham houses have differences, both within and without, from old Brewster houses, and old Sandwich houses have their special characteristics. Not until you get into the specific styles do you find homogeneity.

Small though these differences may be, they lessen the effectiveness of general yardsticks. Some people think there is similarity between Cape houses and those of Connecticut. The relationship is there but it is so distant as to be of little value in understanding one through the other. The two architectural patterns left from about the same starting line, but they went in different directions.

Connecticut architecture was more sophisticated from early on. It had greater access to materials such as lime for mortar, stone, and massive hardwood. It had more money, skill, technical knowledge and experience behind it, and so progressed in a different time frame that was at times as much as a hundred years out of sync with that on the Cape. It was also settled by people from other parts of England, who brought with them regional differences.

Cape Codders were more self-satisfied, more traditional, less ardently concerned with the latest wiggle in fashion. Both they and their Connecticut neighbors did beautiful work, but in their own way.

Tradition is a large factor when it comes to dating old houses. While waiting for a meeting to start one time, I was listening to a woman on my left who had just bought the "oldest house in town." She was in raptures about it. "Built in 1675" said the plaque above the front door, and the lady went into panegyrics about the old wood, the wide floor boards, the low ceilings, the pinning of the rafters and so on.

On my right sat a gentleman who was an Historian of Knowledge. "Only one problem," he rumbled, "that house burned down in 1840." The lady on my left shrank to the size of a Barbie doll.

The gentleman was not only correct, but his comment was an important one. Records of fires are almost never available, and folk did, in 1840, from a strong sense of tradition, build much as people had many years before.

Another lady told me of a great expert from Boston whom she asked to date her house. The Great Expert came into the living room, looked with care at the windows, and said the house clearly was built in the 1750s. He came from areas where people built a house all at once with new-at-that-time materials. The windows did not come from Aunt Minnie's barn, the town dump, and the old house next door, as they do here.

Folks give windows a lot of weight when dating houses. A gentleman whom I did not know called me from New Jersey and said, "The windows in my house in Eastham are thus and so; how old is my house?" I spent some time studying his house later, but never came up with a date, at least nothing that I felt secure about within seventy-five years.

The Cape Codder views his house much as he views his boat — it is a moveable feast and nothing to get dogmatic about. Anyone who lives by the sea is flexible and so must his possessions be.

Which brings us to another complication — the ease and pleasure with which Cape Codders moved their houses. Without utility wires to get in the way, with houses in general being small and oxen strong, houses were moved at will and with little fuss.

Old houses were moved by a process called flaking. The wooden pins used to hold the house frame together were knocked out and the house thus dismantled into its component parts. These were laid flat on a wagon and dragged to the new destination.

Since each piece of the house was numbered at the time of construction, the numbers made it easy to reassemble the building at the new location. Numbering was done here as it had been done in England, using Roman numerals. Roman numbers are composed of straight lines and these are easily made with an axe slash. Britons did not begin to use Arabic numbers until the 1500s.

Moving nailed buildings was also called flaking, but in this case you sawed the house into pieces along the studs and along the rafters. To reassemble you nailed a two-by-four along the raw edges of the house pieces and this gave you a firm base for renailing the entire house together.

In reading old accounts we find that people sometimes gave their house a quarter turn just to change the view or to face the newly made street. I have seen this done several times in the past few years, too. The housewife sometimes got tired of the neighborhood. Since many people owned another bit of land here or there, it was not unusual to pick up the house and take it to another location. Sometimes a house was cut in half and one half moved away.

Houses "from away" also complicate matters. Off-Cape houses, especially from Nantucket, dot the Cape. When whaling fell off and Nantucketers were broke, they might have nothing left to sell but their home. Cape Codders, often poor, might be able to afford such a bargain. Houses brought from the mainland are often more sophisticated and are made of woods that were not available here.

Old maps can deceive you. If the 1858 map shows a lot with no house, but there is a house on that lot five years later, this does nothing to date the house. It could already be a hundred years old and brought from "foreign parts" or from up the street.

To understand your house you must let the house itself tell you its story, and no one part has the starring role. Most of the house must sing the same song.

And on what part of the house should you lean your date? A wonderful lady, owner of a fine old house, told me that her family had built and owned the house since it was built, and that the records were clear that the house had been built in 1817. That was a fairly early date for the town in which she lived, the town not being noted for substantial construction in times past.

Some time later she sold the house and the new owner stripped it down to bare bones, so I had a fine time studying the anatomy. The floor of the Hall had rotted away and under the bits I found evidence that there had been an older Hall. Nothing remained but vestiges, but no doubt there had been a nucleus that the 1817 owner had removed when he built the present domicile.

I did not mention this to the new owner; he was not interested and he promptly declared in a newspaper interview that he had the Oldest House In Town, dating from the early 1700s.

Why contradict him? People are happiest believing what they want to believe, and they will so believe in spite of any evidence to the contrary. At least twenty people have told me that they have "the oldest house in town." Why spoil their pleasure?

Another house looks, both inside and out, to have been built around 1870. It is a handsome Second Gothic Revival and inside are wonderfully coved and hand-stenciled ceilings and many other good-looking things. But down in the cellar we find that the present house was built on a much earlier house, and you can't tell how much of this earlier house is sealed into the walls and structure. So how would you date this?

Please don't take anything I say as gospel. I make plenty of mistakes. My interest in Cape Cod houses was sparked by Dean Arthur Tarbell (who wrote *Cape Cod Ahoy*). In the early 1940s he was giving talks and slide shows to local organizations. I went along and ran his projector. He had a little metal cricket in his hand, and when he clicked this, I would slide the picture from one side of the projector to the other. (That's why they call them "slides.")

His pictures were good and his talk enthusiastic, and our junkets took us into many lovely old homes, but it was some years later that my interest took a serious turn. When I began to read up on Cape architecture I found that much of what had been written was mythology, and the real knowledge was in people and in the houses themselves. Then I started asking questions and next I got an old pair of dungarees and a flashlight and a stepladder. Then I began to learn a little. I still advocate asking questions and looking for answers yourself as the best way to learn about your house.

You will get dirt on your knees and cobwebs in your hair, but talk to your house, and soon it will talk to you.

CHAPTER TWENTY

Looking at old houses—
II. The bits and pieces

To learn about your old house, first go to your Town Office and then to the County Court House. Ask people in your neighborhood about the house. Ask the Historical Society and the Historical Commission for information. Get a notebook and write everything down, even if it is contradictory, even if it sounds crazy. You need as many pieces as possible to make a picture, and who knows which one will be a key piece.

Most of the evidence provided by the house itself is in the cellar and in the attic. Here the structure is still to be seen, and here the fewest changes have been made. Much of the rest of the house is apt to be face paint.

Go down into the cellar. It may be round and of brick; it may be square and of rough-dressed granite blocks; it may be random rubble field stone. Or it may be made of two or three of these materials, showing different times of construction.

Look up at the floor joists. They may have been—to borrow a phrase from the used-car fellers—"pre-used," and maybe more than once. This will be evident through peg holes, nails and mortise cuts that do not pertain to present use.

What can you see of the wall structure? Are the walls studded or are they made of vertical boards? Or both? Is the crawl space from the cellar walls out to the foundation of good size or is it about cat-high, with a few tunnels for the plumber to wiggle along to get to the pipes? Lower foundations tend to belong to older houses, but none of these things are themselves of great significance. We need to total it all up at the end.

What can you see of the chimney stack? Is it large? Are the bricks a delicate pink, suggesting that they are soft and have had little kilning? The stack may be on a brick arch; this indicates fine workmanship and was done off Cape more often than on.

Although Boston had a brick kiln as early as 1636, the method used on Cape was to pile the bricks up into a heap, cover them with brush and fire the whole thing. Those bricks that were well burnt were used for outside work; the ones that were merely pink were soft and they were used indoors or for nogging (i.e., for filling walls as insulation).

A favorite myth for many people is the one about ballast brick. The way it usually goes is that all of the big old buildings in Boston and all of the oldish chimneys and foundations on Cape Cod were built of brick brought from England as ship's ballast. Think about it — and then forget it.

Research done on vessels entering and leaving Boston reveals almost no mention of ballast bricks being dropped off. Here and there a private party shipped in a cargo of bricks, but rarely. Some bricks did come into Newport, but none were loaded on an oxcart and dragged to the Cape. Moreover, transatlantic vessels put into Boston, not into Wellfleet or Brewster.

During Norman times, in Britain, brick size was twelve inches by four inches by three and a quarter inches. In 1625, under King Charles the first, English law established the legal size of brick to be nine inches by four and a half inches by three inches. In the New England Colonies the Charter of 1692 also dictated brick size to be nine inches by four and a half inches by three inches. In addition the Charter required the Selectmen of every town in Massachusetts Bay, which included Cape Cod, to appoint a "suitable person" to inspect the molds used in making bricks and to enforce the size regulations.

People did, however — especially on Cape where supervision

was a bit less stringent — make smaller bricks than legal size; they sometimes made them larger too, but the smaller bricks fired more readily.

The Charter of 1692 is well worth reading for its own sake. It gives explicit rules for making bricks in the New England Colonies. The clay must be "digged" before December 19 and placed where it can be trampled by cattle. (They had no pug mills in those days; besides, the cattle added straw and other valuable ingredients.) The clay must be turned over in the month of March, "at least twenty days before it be wrought. No person shall temper his clay with brackish water nor dig his clay in any place where salt water comes in."

That really remarkable Charter had a finger in every aspect of Colonial life, discussing how to care for posthumous children, sexual relations of all kinds, and the number of shingles in a bundle, and instructing the Selectmen in each Town to be sure that the Tithing Man's wand had a brass tip of six inches.

A question to ask yourself while you are still in the cellar is, where does the trap door rise? Into the Keeping Room or into the Hall? The latter might indicate that the Hall was built first. Watch your floor boards. They can tell you where old partitions were, where rooms were added and added to, and sometimes the location of an old hearth.

What mattered to old-timers in regard to floor boards was that the boards should run from wall to wall without a break. The most fashionable width was eight inches, with ten or twelve inches being acceptable. If there were a mill and the money to get the floor boards run through, that is what happened. It happened less often on the Lower Cape than on the Upper.

They only used wide boards when they had to. For you and for me, wide boards are associative. We look at them and our mind's eye visualizes "the forest primeval, the murmuring pines and the hemlocks." But Longfellow did not write "Evangeline" until 1847, at which time everything had a romantic coloration.

To the early settlers, the vast wilderness and the great trees with the slender deer ghosting through them were terrifying challenges, not mawkish ideals.

You did want a really wide board for above the hearth, and you got this from off Cape. Anything else of width was put into the walls for quicker construction and fewer draughts. Leftovers went into the attic floor. Had there been a demand from off Cape for wide boards, Cape Codders would have sold them gladly, if they had had them. The Cape is not in the White Pine Belt.

The doors and windows have two potential values. One is that handmade doors and windows are a joy in themselves, but again, it is associative. You picture the Man of the House, sitting by the fire of a winter's evening, whittling out the pegs to put together the doors and the windows, and then feather-edging the door panels. But you can't see the weary lines on his face or that he has just cut his thumb. He wished that he could buy doors.

Secondly, if many aspects of the house are in agreement as to construction, and the doors and windows reinforce this, that gives them a large value. Or you may have five different types of windows, some from the town dump, some from Aunt Sarah's barn, and so on. Windows have no significance in themselves for dating.

Houses seldom show evidence of previous windows, because each set was larger than the preceding one. Old houses often have had three or four sets, and those sliders of yours make five.

Check out the latches and hinges and the holes in the door where latches once were. Look for signs of handmade hardware. There may be old latch marks around those fancy new door knobs.

The Revolution was a big cut-off date for Cape building. Through the hard years of the Revolution, building here was an impossibility. The Cape was poor, and every beef, every blanket and every man that the Cape could spare was recruited. When these had all gone, the Cape was asked to give more.

Trade stopped, fishing boats rotted on the beach and for ten years times were tough. When the men got back, it took some while to re-establish a constructive life. But those men who came home had seen something of the mainland; they saw sash windows, they saw bake ovens conveniently placed on the side of the hearth rather than at the back. And when their wives heard about these new fashions — guess what?

So after the Revolution and as soon as men could get to building homes for "the girls they had left behind them," casement windows went out the door and the new sash windows were installed. That miserable oven at the back of the hearth was covered over and a new side oven made. Now you didn't have to duck your head to creep to the oven and come out with soot in your hair anyway. And mantel shelves made the scene now, too.

How about the woodwork in your house? Is it handmade or machined? If you can see into the walls anywhere, perhaps in a closet, are there studs? Are they commercial two-by-fours or strange pieces of odds and ends, which, of course, would be an older type of building material. And look at the walls on both levels. Don't assume that either level came first. Many Cape houses have been built by raising a small house up in the air and putting a new ground floor beneath it.

Can you find laths that key plaster? See if they are machined or handmade (machined will of course be regular, handmade will be irregular), or is accordion lath used? Accordion lath was a common makeshift done by taking a wide board and slitting it, not quite all the way, alternating the slits first at one end and then at the other, and then spreading the board as wide as possible so that the slits keyed the plaster.

And now, looking at the wood itself, you can probably find wood in your house that has been cut in several different ways. The modern circular saw makes marks that, like the music, go round and round. The manual saw that you keep in the workshop, being powered by the human arm, makes slightly irregular kerf marks of considerable swath. The kerf marks made by the water-powered, up-and-down sawmill are regular and close together and at right angles to the length of the board. Wood cut by sawmill was available off Cape after the mid 1700s, but was slower reaching the Cape. Then there was the pit saw, a method used by the Romans two thousand years ago and used in American factories through the 1800s.

The pit saw gave a slanted kerf mark because if the man at the bottom of the pit (the "under dog") had stood directly below his buddy, he would not have been able to see a thing, with all the saw dust in his eyes. I suspect that he closed his eyes a lot anyway.

Beams and boards can also be made with a broadaxe and smoothed with an adze. An adze makes a beautifully smooth board with little dips in it that catch tiny shadows. I know a house that was built in 1825, where the boards, wall and floor were smoothed by an adze. The love and patience employed in that method is hard to imagine today. It is delightful but, again, only through association. It thrills us, but it must have been a deuce of a lot of work for that proud young householder.

Without meaning to be difficult, I must say that whatever way or ways the wood in your house was sawn does not supply a date. It only adds to the picture. Old boards might have been introduced from another house and newer boards might be merely a recent addition.

The stairs and the way they evolved give clues. Hand holds on the wall came first, then a ladder, next flat treads without risers, then a straight run of closed string stairs, then open string stairs and then two or more runs. Flat-sawn balusters preceded turned balusters. And when were the stairs constructed or changes made in them? This depends on your neighborhood and on the financial and personal attitude of the builder.

If the house is a storey and a half, look behind the knee wall upstairs. Is the plate flush with the floor or does it carry ten or so inches above the floor level? Is the knee wall made of full-size two-by-fours or made of scraps? In the attic, are the rafters bowed and by how much? Is there a ridge pole and how do the rafters meet?

Is the ridge pole, if there is one, an unpeeled log? In the attic you should be able to see more of the construction of the walls.

Outside, let's look at the foundation. This will probably show the original building and several additions. It may be made of rough-dressed granite or bricks. Cement blocks that have been molded with a rough texture came in the 1920s and after.

Do the window frames jut out from the wall, indicating that the walls are or were too thin to enclose them, with the exterior boarding slap up against the interior woodwork?

Measure the spacing between one window and another and between the windows and the door. This may show that one side of the facade was built to a different mensuration than the other, suggesting that a small house was enlarged. Sometimes a house is wonderfully consistent in so many things, and other times you get an exciting feeling of growth and change as you move around.

Take all of your information and ask yourself WHY? Look at the houses in your neighborhood or similar houses in your town. How does yours fit in? Get some friends to "do" their houses too, and compare. This is an immense amount of fun. But the really important thing is that this is your house. Enjoy it.

Supplementary reading

Benjamin, Asher. *The American Builder's Companion.* New York: Dover Publications, 1969.

Boswell's Journal of a Tour to the Hebrides with Samuel Johnson LLD., 1773. New York: Yale University Press, McGraw-Hill Book Company, 1967, pp. 99–100, 137, 219–220.

Braun, Hugh. *Old English Houses.* London: Faber and Faber Ltd., 1962.

Downing, Andrew Jackson. *The Architecture of Country Houses.* New York: Dover Publications, 1969.

Downing, Antoinette, and Scully, Vincent, Jr. *The Architectural Heritage of Newport, Rhode Island.* New York: Bramhall House, 1952.

Fletcher, Sir Banister. *A History of Architecture on the Comparative Method.* New York: Charles Scribner's Sons, 1924.

Fowler, Orson S. *The Octagon, A Home For All.* New York: Dover Publications, 1973.

Innocent, Charles F. *The Development of English Building Construction.* Devon, England: Charles and David Reprints, 1971.

Kilham, Walter H. *Boston After Bullfinch.* Cambridge: Harvard University Press, 1946.

Kimball, Fiske. *Domestic Architecture of the American Colonies and of the Early Republic.* New York: Dover Publications, 1966.

Luckiesh, M. *Visual Illusions, Their Causes, Characteristics and Applications.* New York: Dover Publications, 1973.

Martin, George. *Fences, Gates and Bridges, A Practical Manual.* Brattleboro, Vt.: Stephen Greene Press, 1974.

Palladio, Andrea. *The Four Books of Architecture.* New York: Dover Publications, 1965.

Saylor, Henry H. *Bungalows.* Philadelphia: John C. Winston, 1913.

Sloan, Eric. *An Age of Barns.* New York: Ballantine Books, 1974.

Sloan, Eric. *A Museum of Early American Tools.* New York: Ballantine Books, 1973.

Van Rensselaer, Mariana Griswold. *Henry Hobson Richardson and His Works.* New York: Dover Publications, 1969.

Vaux, Calvert. *Villas and Cottages.* New York: Dover Publications, 1970.

Vetruvius. *The Ten Books of Architecture.* Translated by Morris Hickey Morgan. New York: Dover Publications, 1960.

Whiffen, Marcus. *American Architecture Since 1780: A Guide to the Styles.* Cambridge: MIT Press, 1969.

Wood, Margaret. *The English Mediaeval House.* London: Bracken Books, 1983.

Index

Page numbers in **boldface** type indicate the location of the author's drawings; those in *italic*, photographic illustrations.